THE POWER OF POSITIVE PROPHECY

THE POWER OF POSITIVE PROPHECY

How to Envision and Create your Best Future

Alan Vaughan

Aquarian/Thorsons
An Imprint of HarperCollins*Publishers*

The Aquarian Press
A Division of HarperCollins*Publishers*
77–85 Fulham Palace Road,
Hammersmith, London W6 8JB

First published as *The Edge of Tomorrow*
by Coward, McCann, USA, 1982
This edition, revised and updated, 1991

3 5 7 9 10 8 6 4 2

A catalogue record for this book
is available from the British Library

ISBN 1-85538-099-4

Typeset by Burns & Smith Ltd, Derby
Printed in Great Britain by
Mackays of Chatham, Kent

Dedicated to the future and those who will create it—including my children: Lauren, Thomas and Jonathan who will be 23, 21 and 19 when the third millennium dawns on 1 January 2001.

Yesterday is only a dream and tomorrow is but a vision. Yet, each today, well lived, makes every yesterday a dream of happiness and each tomorrow a vision of hope.

—From an ancient Sanskrit proverb

Contents

Acknowledgements

My grateful thanks to the following organizations for their help in study, teaching, learning and research:

The Parapsychology Foundation, New York; The Central Premonitions Registry, New York; The Parapsychological Association, world-wide; in Europe: The Society for Psychical Research, London; The College of Psychic Studies, London; The Parapsychology Institute of the State University of Utrecht, Holland; The Institute for the Border Areas of Psychology, Freiburg, Germany; in New York: The Dream Laboratory of the Maimonides Medical Center, Brooklyn; The American Society for Psychical Research; The City College of New York; Human Dimensions Institute, Buffalo; in California: Humanistic Psychology Program, Sonoma State College; Institute for the Study of Consciousness, Berkeley; Psychic Integration Institute; Stanford Research Institute; The Washington Research Center; The Parapsychology Research Group; UCLA Neuropsychiatric Institute; The Southern California Society for Psychical Research; and the Mobius Society.

Introduction to the Revised Edition

Using the power of positive prophecy in our role of self-visionary may be the key to living up to our potential. For if we cannot envision ourselves making great accomplishments, we will not be able to make them. On a global level, if we cannot envision a world that works, we will not be able to create it. If readers of this book glimpse their own prophetic potential and then strive to make their positive predictions come true, they will not only have proven that intuition works for them, they will have created a private world that works.

If people want to remain skeptical of their own intuitive gifts, it is likely that they will be surprised at how easily their hopes and wishes can be crushed by cruel circumstance. Like the NASA executives who okayed the *Challenger* launch, they will be forcefully reminded of the limitations of logic. Like stockbrokers on 'Black Monday', 19 October 1987, they will feel a sinking feeling in their stomachs and wonder why the financial newsletters did not predict the stock market crash.

No matter how well human affairs are planned, there are always unforeseen events that shape them. It is learning to foresee some of those 'unforseeable' events that this book is all about.

But foreseeing and trying to prevent the disasters of life are only the beginning. The most telling use of our prophetic gift is to create in our minds a masterpeice of future living. Never mind that we seldom fulfill our visions' every promise. That is part of the human condition. But certainly, no one ever achieved anything worthwhile without beginning with a vision that inspired the reality.

To make this book really work for you, you must be brave enough to attempt some of the exercises. The worst you can be is wrong. That should give you the impetus to try it again. If you make enough mistakes, you will learn quickly—and finally begin to get it right. Keep in mind that there is no sin in being wrong—you may be seeing a future that does not happen. If you focus your predictions on positive outcomes in your own life, you will also have the satisfaction of self-fulfilling your own prophecy. That's not cheating—just creating your own best reality.

This edition is considerably revised and enlarged from the first edition, entitled *The Edge of Tomorrow*. I have added two new chapters, 'Personal Dream Prophecy' and 'Making Prophecy Practical', updated throughout, and deleted the chapter on the Central Premonitions Registry, which has ceased operation.

Alan Vaughan
Los Angeles
September 1990

Introduction to the First Edition

When I began to investigate precognition in 1966, it was a purely scientific endeavour. I wanted to know if it was possible to see into the future. And if so, how?

I believe I have found the answers. But what I did not expect to find was that this very search for the answer to the riddle of humanity and time should reveal a new insight into how we can transform our lives through foreseeing our best potentials and fulfilling them.

For me, the search has been a personal transformation—from a skeptical science editor to the person many people call 'the world's most accurate psychic predictor'. By trying to find out how the prophetic mind functions, I inadvertently became an expert practitioner of the prophetic arts.

In a 1973 book, *Patterns of Prophecy*, I told the story of my early search for proof that accurate prediction of human events is possible. I developed the theory that each of us has a *blueprint of life*, much like our physical DNA blueprint, which contains the seeds of our future. I concluded that our minds do not travel in time like a time machine, but rather perceive glimpses of blueprints of future events. Our actions and choices—our free will—determine which of these blueprinted futures becomes reality.

A 1979 book of mine, *Incredible Coincidence*, made the point that we all seem to possess unconscious foreknowledge of our blueprints and that all of us are psychically linked in a complex dovetailing of blueprints which results in meaningful coincidence. I also set forth a theory of how consciousness creates reality, space, time and matter by influencing chance events.

The Power of Positive Prophecy draws on my breakthrough research into precognition to show how we can foresee and fulfill our futures. My theory is refined so that it can be tested in the laboratory and in life; it is the first verifiable general theory of psychic phenomena.

By the word *psychic* I do not mean the media stereotype of a person who has mysterious powers others do not have. The 'media psychic' foresees disasters, issues warnings about earthquakes, has virtual omniscience about celebrities, politics and football scores. This stereotype must be able to solve murders, find missing persons and tell people how to solve all their problems. He or she should have a hotline to God, spirit guides, UFO entities, or at least *something* mysterious and baffling—and at the very least, should be able to see auras, ghosts, and invisible entities. Some people fit this media stereotype very well, indeed carry it off with flair. But it is not what I have in mind.

The phenomena the media psychic displays become trivial when compared with what I believe all of us can learn to do: free our minds from skepticism and put our psychic talents to work to fulfill our lives and our future.

In my own experience I have found the most powerful tool of transformation to be dreams. By glimpsing positive futures in my own life, by training what I call my *dream tiger*, I have found that dreams can provide a channel for the inner self to express its highest hopes and hold forth promises that our conscious minds can work to keep.

I recall having a childhood dream that terrified me, yet offered a promise. In the dream, which I had many times between the ages of eight and twelve, I saw myself as a hairy, frightening wolfman. Someone loaded a gun with a silver bullet melted from a cross and shot me through the heart—on Easter Sunday. But the bullet did not kill me because deep inside I was good.

As a boy I thought the dream meant merely that I had been watching too many horror movies. But now I realize that it was a *transformation dream*. In a symbolic way the dream stated that the promise of Easter—death and resurrection—is for us while we are alive. Our lower natures can be transformed through spiritual death and rebirth. When our animal heritage yields to the promptings of the inner self, our higher natures can emerge to direct our extraordinary creative powers. We are all waiting for the rebirth of that 'good' inside.

For me, personally, the dream symbolically predicted the events of an Easter Sunday in 1972 when, in a mystical flash of insight, I suddenly realized the power of prophecy to create future reality. It has taken me a long time to put this realization to use. My wolfman nature, seen that day as a cartoon, still puts up a fight. But the cross transformed into a bullet did pierce my animal heart.

In looking back at my prophetic experiences, I recognize a typical pattern. Premonitory dream warnings begin the pattern. Since our psychic inner selves have developed an early-warning system through biological evolution, many people never progress beyond the loudest psychic signals warning of death and disaster. But with training and effort, premonitions can be converted into dream promises.

The second stage is one of questioning, of seeking out teachers, of experimenting and trying to tame the wild talent of prophecy. In my developing years I gave many psychic readings for people, attempting to sense what lay ahead for them. Over the years I have received much feedback from these readings—enough to know that I was sometimes able to read the true blueprints of a person's future. At other times I would fail by giving in to the impulse to tell people what they hoped to hear.

The third stage begins with teaching others how to nurture their psychic talents for use in their own lives. In the process of teaching, of course, one learns even more: how individuals differ in their ways of relating to the psychic world of images and how different approaches work with different people. Yet by trying various approaches to psychic unfoldment, I have found that most people can find a way that works for them.

If this sounds like a painless path to perfection, I have given you the wrong idea. Mistakes, hard lessons, disappointments, unfulfilled promises and not a few heartbreaks undercut this path as much as any other. But I think we learn more by overcoming difficulties. When we realize that our mistakes belong to us—and can become our best teachers—we can quickly integrate their lessons into our lives without repeating them.

My purpose in writing this book is to provide you with tools to glimpse your future promise, your potentials, abilities, and talents. By holding up a mirror to your inner self, you can glimpse how best to proceed with fulfilling your dreams.

The practical nuts-and-bolts problems of life and society need solutions, which can come only from individuals who are using their heightened powers of future awareness. I include techniques and suggestions for everyday future consciousness as well as foreseeing the larger picture of society. I present not more proof of precognition, but ways to find the answer that works best.

If my techniques are to work for most people, they should have the broadest testing base possible. For that reason I discuss a number of scientific experiments with a wide variety of human subjects—the so-called average person. The value of these experiments is that they show how things work for *most* people in the long run.

Each chapter concludes with step-by-step exercises for readers who want to go beyond merely knowing *how* to foresee and fulfill their futures, who have the motivation actually to *do* it.

If this book fulfills my own dreams for it, it will help you to realize that precognition is a natural function of human consciousness, not a strange mysterious, and baffling oddity. If my theory is right, each living being *has* to be capable of seeing into the future and fulfilling that prophecy. The cornerstone of my system lies in belief—not only that precognition is possible but *that you can do it*. You may never find that steadfast core of belief until you try to do it and personally experience your talent of foreknowledge.

As you try the various exercises in future consciousness, keep in mind that the worst you can do is be wrong. Don't try to convince your skeptical friends of your powers—they have to convince themselves—but concentrate on predicting events that have meaning for you. You have only one hypothesis to test: can you put your prophetic talents to work to foresee and help fulfill *your* best future? If, day by day, as the edge of tomorrow becomes the now of today, and the past of yesterday, and you find your nows becoming better than they were, you will know that you have found the way to tame your wild talent of prophecy.

The final chapter envisions a future time in which our children learn to use *consciousness technology* to create a better society. It is my prophecy that the third millennium will dawn over a time of unprecedented evolutionary advance in which we master our latent powers of mind to fulfill human dreams.

1.

Believing the Impossible

To achieve the impossible one must first believe that the impossible is possible. Once we believed it was possible to run a four-minute mile or go to the moon, we were able to do it. According to classical physics, seeing into the future is clearly impossible. Yet there are persistent claims of people actually doing it. If we can show that precognition is a well-proven fact, then we can believe in it—and disbelieve in the adequacy of classical physics.

Published Predictions

The average person's awareness of psychic predictions comes from tabloid newspapers. Would-be believers, however, will be sorely disappointed if they depend on the published predictions of the tabloid psychics for accurate precognition. Evaluating 360 predictions made by 10 psychics in the *National Enquirer* for the years 1976–9, *The Book of Predictions* (1981) found that each of four psychics had one prediction right and six had none right.[1] In total, these psychics were 98.9 per cent *wrong*. Even the hits were not impressive: two chose the winning presidential candidate, one predicted a celebrity marriage and one predicted a celebrity divorce.

If you are thinking that you could probably score higher than that in making predictions, you are only probably right—but you may be taking an important first step in the art of prediction.

But how on earth could people get reputations as psychics and be so wrong as the 10 *Enquirer* psychics? I know four of them and am familiar with the work of two others, and, without naming names, I feel that most of them are genuine psychics when it comes to getting impressions for clients. But when an *Enquirer* reporter calls them up and asks them about a list of celebrities with whom they have no contact, they bomb out just as easily as anyone else.

Not being without sin, I shall cast no stone at the *Enquirer* psychics, however. My own predictions were run by the *National Enquirer* on 23 May 1971.[2] A Cheshire, Connecticut, newsman named Henry Chase analyzed the predictions of five psychics published in the *Enquirer* in 1971 and found mine most accurate (54.5 per cent right). Chase had predicted that no one would score above 10 per cent. Judge for yourself if my predictions warrant any belief in precognition. My comments are in brackets.

- There will be a strong upsurge in the national economy within the next few weeks. [Logical prediction, which can be discounted.]
- FBI director J. Edgar Hoover will resign by the end of the summer (1971). [Wrong. He died in 1972.]
- US involvement in Vietnam and the military draft will end by the middle of next year (1972). [Both predictions right.]
- President Nixon will be reelected. [Right.]
- Senator Edward M. Kennedy will become president in 1976. [Wrong.]
- A financial scandal connected with Wall Street and with people close to Nixon will occur during his second term. [Partially right: Agnew's resignation because of financial scandal and the Watergate scandal.]
- Mrs Jacqueline Kennedy Onassis will become a widow again, probably by the end of 1973. [Wrong, it was 1975.]
- The United States and Russia will join forces to explore the outer planets. [Wrong so far. But Russian and US scientists are now discussing a possible joint flight to Mars.]
- Reverend Philip Berrigan, Roman Catholic priest accused of an alleged plot against the government, will be exonerated. [Right.]
- Mount Pelée, a long-dormant volcano on the Caribbean island of Martinique, will erupt by 1972. [Wrong.]
- Severe flooding will hit northern New Jersey and parts of New York City within two years. [Right. In June 1972, Hurricane Agnes dumped 28 trillion gallons of water on eastern states, including New Jersey and New York, causing the most costly disaster in American history.]

My reckoning agrees with that of Henry Chase's: 54.5 per cent right.

In recent years the *Enquirer* editors have taken to making up ridiculous, if entertaining, predictions about celebrities and running them under the names of psychics. So the *Enquirer* no longer provides a forum for actual psychic predictions in its year-end and mid-year cover stories.

Personal Predictions

Belief in precognition usually comes from personal experience or the experiences of people known to you. Such belief rarely comes to the skeptic. But there are exceptions—I am one. When I began research into precognition in 1966 I was a skeptical science editor of college texts. Yet I was troubled by what seemed to be psychic experiences. Obtaining a grant from the Parapsychology Foundation, I journeyed to Europe for a two-year research project.

Belief forced itself on me as I became the target for about a hundred psychic readings by psychics, mediums, fortune-tellers, card readers, crystal gazers and astrologers—a veritable zoo of soothsayers. Their psychic abilities varied enormously. Much of what they said was too vague to be a hit, but occasionally a few of them would zero in with considerable detail about some event in my life. Most impressive to me were those predictions that came as a surprise to me but actually happened years later.

As an example of what I consider a reasonably good psychic reading, consider a session with a British psychic in London on 25 August 1967. Looking like a portly Irish squire, he is famous for his ghost hunts and has written several books. It is something of a shock when he reveals his crystal ball, asks you to rub oil on your hands and transfer it to the crystal, then tells you to shut up while he gazes into the crystal and tells your fortune. He repeats this with special cards. He would not permit a tape recording so I took these notes of his predictions.

1. September and October will be the most important months in my life. [Not that I noticed.]
2. I will get a lot of help from an older man who has trouble with his spine and talks loudly. Initials are C.F.G. [Not so far.]
3. I shall be commissioned to travel and I shall travel quite a lot. [A good hit.]
4. It looks like books around me. [This is my fifth book.]
5. I ought to write on the occult or ESP. [I have, beginning in 1969.]

6. My writing could be serialized. [Several magazines and newspapers have reprinted segments of several of my books.]
7. I am going to change homes and states as well. [I have, from New York to California.]
8. I am going to live in a house that overlooks a narrow expanse of water. [A good hit: from 1980 to 1982 I lived in a house on the bank of the Los Angeles River, a narrow river if there ever was one.]
9. I am going to write something that could be made into a film. [Four other psychics made the same prediction. I recently wrote a movie script that is being considered for production.]
10. A legal contract is not far away. [My first book contract was five years away.]
11. Real estate profits come in later. [It must be *very* much later.]
12. I shall talk with Eastern people, Japanese and Chinese. [I did, a great deal, years later when living in San Francisco.]
13. Europe will be important to me. [Vague but true.]
14. A magazine will send me somewhere on the other side of the Atlantic (i.e., the United States). [A good hit, since beginning in 1969 through 1977 I frequently traveled on assignments for *Psychic* magazine.]

Over half of those predictions I consider hits. The other half are too vague or not distinctive enough or are wrong so far. The psychic knew nothing about me, nor did he even look at me after he told me to keep quiet, so he was not picking up sensory information from me. But even if he had, he was telling me about things in the future that I did not know about. The British psychics were making a believer out of me.

Fortune-Tellers

At the bottom of the credibility scale are the fortune-tellers who inhabit fairs and carnivals. Their predictions are mostly memorized cold readings (readings that apply to everyone), with little hint of the psychic. I once did an experiment with a fortune-teller, an English society woman who read cards for about 25 people at a charity affair. The fortune-teller agreed to my proposal to interview all her clients after their readings and record her predictions. About halfway through the experiment it dawned on me that she was not only making extremely vague predictions that would apply to nearly everyone ('You will cross water soon', 'You will be attending a wedding soon'), but she was giving half the people the *same* predictions.

To be fair, I should report another experiment done by a New Jersey researcher, Emily P. Cary.[3] Visiting 15 fortune-tellers—the five-dollar variety—in New Jersey and New York, Cary found no evidence of ESP. But her last-chance visit to Miss Polly, in Summit, New Jersey, yielded not only a casting director's dream—'the original ancient crony of Romany'—but also some quite accurate psychic impressions about herself, her husband, and her two boys. She resisted the temptation to pay 25 dollars for predictions about her *next* life, but at least she found one fortune-teller who actually was psychic. Odds of 16 to 1 make a visit to a fortune-teller unlikely to produce psychic results. Worse, fortune-tellers tend to be con artists looking for susceptible clients out of whom they milk thousands of dollars with extravagant promises of bringing luck, fame and fortune, removing curses, or returning lost lovers.

A man recently related to me his experience with a New York fortune-teller. She announced that he had a curse on him and she would require 5,000 dollars to remove it. He suggested a little experiment in which he would give her 500 dollars for the first part of the ritual to remove the curse. If nothing happened, he would have his money refunded. Ringed in lit candles, she held a pigeon over his head. She killed the pigeon with a knife and let the blood drip over his head. A few days later he complained to her that nothing had changed and he wanted his money back. She shrugged and said that she had donated it all to the church. He didn't believe that, but his 'little experiment' left him with an expensive lesson: don't trust gypsy fortune-tellers.

I hasten to add that there are hundreds of legitimate psychics. They don't make extravagant claims. A *National Directory of Psychic Counselors* now being compiled by Elizabeth Nelson (Carma Press, Box 12633, St Paul, MN 55112, USA) has over 600 psychics recommended by their colleagues. Also over 800 psychics in 49 states and other countries are listed in *Where Are The Psychics?* by Miriam Larsen (Box 3008, Garland, TX 75047–3008, USA).

Seeing is Believing

My transition from skeptic to believer to amateur and now professional psychic came in steps, based on what I observed other psychics do and what experimenters asked me to try in their laboratories. Like all arts, the psychic arts are based on belief by experience: seeing is believing, hearing is believing, psychic sensing is believing. The type of psychic work I do now requires a precision I did not believe possible 15 years ago. Yet because I have seen others do it, I have tried it and found it *is* possible.

A technique used by a number of researchers to induce belief in ESP in their subjects is simply to demonstrate previous successes by others. If subjects are willing to believe that they might be able to do it, half the battle is won.

In my classes and seminars I demonstrate ESP before asking the students to attempt it. For instance, at a recent seminar I pointed to a young man named Fred and said, 'Now, if I were giving a psychic reading. I might say, "Fred lives on a farm with 30 cows and one goat." And then Fred would say, "That's not bad. I live on a farm with 30 cows but we have no goat." 'At that point an excited Fred exclaimed, 'But I *do* live on a farm, and we *do* have 30 cows, and we *don't* have a goat.'

'See what I mean?' I said. And the belief generated among my students seemed a factor in their subsequent success at doing readings. Sometimes just an open mind and a desire for psychic experience is enough to trigger it.

In working with several thousand students over the years, I find that usually over 95 per cent of them are successful in demonstrating ESP when attempting psychic readings for each other. My technique is to divide them into pairs and ask them to make statements about each other. The students usually give their partners a higher rating than themselves, indicating they have lingering doubts about their own abilities.

Sometimes the results are clear-cut. For example, a woman held a ring belonging to her partner and stated, 'All I can think of is the Honolulu Hilton.' Her partner laughed, 'But I bought the ring at the Honolulu Hilton!'

A recent poll by priest-sociologist Andrew Greeley of the University of Chicago National Opinion Poll showed that so-called 'paranormal' experiences are now the norm.[4] A full two-thirds of American adults report psychic experiences. This finding startled Greeley since was such an enormous increase over polls from earlier years.

Among establishment scientists, however, belief in ESP remains low. The most skeptical group are the psychologists. One reason for this might be that their research might be explained as resulting from ESP, and not from their theories. I can't say I blame them for their panic and their often cold rejection of psychic research. If you had built your life's reputation on, say, psychological testing and discovered that these tests could be significantly influenced by someone sitting in the next room concentrating on the answers, wouldn't you panic?

When I met two psychologists whose research showed exactly those results, I asked them when their work would be published. Growing red in the face, one psychologist said, 'When the experiment is replicated.' It seemed such a daring departure from classical psychology that the researchers feared for their reputations lest someone else confirm their results. That was finally done, and their research was published a few years later.

When polls have asked people about belief in the various types of extra-sensory perception, answers show a consistent preference for belief in telepathy over precognition. Seeing into the future seems to most people to be more impossible than sensing others' thoughts.

Déjà Vu

In a poll of actual psychic experience, however, well over 80 per cent of respondents claimed that they had experienced the phenomenon of *déjà vu* (French for 'already seen', seeming to experience something for a second time). I agree with a number of parapsychologists who feel that *déjà vu* represents the reactivated memory of a forgotten precognitive dream to achieve that puzzling experience of having done something before. *Déjà vu* is the most common kind of psychic experience.

Some psychologists offer alternate theories for *déjà vu*. A theory proposed a century ago—before psychic phenomena were being studied—suggested that sensory input is processed by one half of the brain before the other, achieving an illusion of remembering twice. This theory has proponents today, but they have no excuse for ignoring the cases in which the person experiencing *déjà vu* is able to predict the conclusion of the event.

Although no one has been able to trigger *déjà vu* at will in the laboratory, it is such a universal experience that psychologists do not deny its existence—they only explain it away as illusory. If you, like the majority of people, have experienced *déjà vu*, you have a personal reason for believing in the possibility of precognition.

Think about your own *déjà vu* experiences. Was there anything uncanny about them? Did they leave you with a strange feeling?

Were you able to predict what someone was going to say or do next? Did you have the feeling that you had dreamed about the events before? You be the judge of whether your brain was playing tricks or whether something *very strange* happened. You may find a foundation for believing in the impossible.

My father was highly skeptical of psychic phenomena until my researches into it finally convinced him that it was possible. He then told me an interesting story of *déjà vu* that happened when he was a teenager. Standing at a railway crossing on a narrow street, he suddenly was overwhelmed by the feeling that it had happened before. As he noted the serial number of the freight car going by, he inexplicably 'knew' what the serial number of the next car would be. As the next car rolled into view—with the correct serial number, not related to that of the earlier car—a shudder of recognition passed through him. During the many years he maintained a skeptical view of psychic phenomena, the memory of this precognitive *déjà vu* was suppressed.

Unconscious ESP

For me, belief in psychic phenomena began at age 30. Yet, in reviewing my early life for hints of ESP experience, I, too, found that I had suppressed some memories. While in college I had read a book by J.B. Rhine on ESP card guessing but was skeptical of the claimed results. Perhaps, as some critics charged, Rhine was playing around with statistics? To put the matter of the test, I attempted to guess the number of 40 ordinary playing cards, 4 suits of ace through 10. I held each card face down for a moment, made my guess and recorded it, then put the card face down in a pile without feedback. When I compared my guesses with the cards, I was utterly shocked. There were 12 hits, including 7 in a row—against highly significant odds (4 right would be expected by chance). A shiver passed through me. I was spooked.

The next day I repeated the experiment—with no hits—and quickly buried this upsetting experience in my subconscious for many years. If you have a firm disbelief in the impossible, experiencing it can be painful indeed.

When unconscious ESP mainifests itself in life, we call it 'luck' or 'coincidence' and dismiss it. I recall a multiple-choice test I had to take in the army. A passing grade meant an additional 50 dollars a month in pay, so the outcome was more than academic. I was worried because I was the only person taking the test in a highly technical subject who had not taken the course in the subject; nor did I have any experience in it. Of the 35 people who took the test that day, I was the first to finish. My speed came not from proficiency but because I couldn't even understand the questions, much less choose the answers in a rational way. So I just swiftly checked off answers at random. When the scores came in I was pleasantly shocked to find that next to the instructor of the course I had the highest grade. What luck! Or was I using ESP in an unconscious way? It paid off with that extra 50 dollars a month.

Sheep and Goats

One of the most durable experimental findings of parapsychology shows that those who believe in psychic phenomena (called 'sheep') score above chance in ESP tests; those who disbelieve ('goats') score below chance. First discovered in the 1940s by New York City College researcher Gertrude Schmeidler, this sheep-goat dichotomy has stood up over the years in tests at many laboratories by many researchers. Happily, though, it is becoming more and more difficult to find proper goats to undertake experiments.

Deviations from chance expectation constitute the measure of ESP forced-choice tests. For instance, if you guess heads or tails when someone flips a coin 10 times, and you guessed five right, that is chance level. If you guessed all 10 right, odds against chance are 1,024 to 1, meaning that you would have to repeat your experiment 1,024 times before you would get all 10 right just by chance, and that you are probably psychic. If you guessed all 10 wrong, you are also probably psychic—since the odds are still 1,024 to 1—but you are using your ESP to avoid the target. The deviations from chance expectation are the same.

If the same trend holds over a great number of trials, we become more certain that ESP is operating, either positively or negatively. Skeptics or goats tend to demonstrate negative ESP, apparently thinking that their low scores disprove ESP.

In an encounter with a Nobel Prize-winning physicist, I was astonished when he said that the concept of negative ESP was nonsense. 'The guesses are just plain wrong,' he said. You might call the physicist a superskeptic, since his emotional response to ESP is so negative that he abandons the logic of science. He will talk blithely about antimatter, but anti-ESP seems nonsense to him because it would wreck his theories about physics. We do not easily yield up beliefs in fondly held theories, especially if they are our bread and butter.

In an experiment in Iceland it was found that people who do *not* read books about psychic phenomena display an impressive ability to score below chance in precognition tests.[5] Those who do read books about ESP (such as you) showed a significant tendency to score positively with precognition. This dichotomy proved to be a more accurate indicator of whether a person would score above or below chance than did the traditional sheep-goat division. Developing an interest in reading about precognition might well presage the actual development of precognitive ability.

An eminent physicist who has bitterly attacked parapsychology has a whole box of books on psychic phenomena in his office, but he has never ready any of them. If his scientific curiosity should ever overcome his emotional bias against psychic phenomena, and he should one day actually read about the phenomena he so heartily rejects out of hand, he might find himself turning into a good subject for precognition experiments. Then, of course, he will be faced with the ugly dilemma of what to do about all those theories in physics that do not accommodate the facts of parapsychology. He can believe in black holes without any trouble—even though there is only sparse evidence for them—but he can't believe that human beings can see into the future without having to admit that the whole theory of modern physics is but a special case, as Newtonian physics proved to be a special case when Einstein's theory of relative space and time displaced it as the ultimate (so far) description of reality.

It will be a painful transition for physicists to encompass a new theory of reality that not only accommodates psychic phenomena but is actually based on them.

If the science Establishment should ever achieve belief in precognition, it might enable scientists to transcend the present limitations of a constricted reality—a reality that conforms to their beliefs.

Finding the Miraculous

Of far greater importance to us than what the science Establishment believes is what we, as individuals, believe. It is quite possible that we have been experiencing the miraculous all along but did not realize it. Our Western education has blinded us to events we cannot explain by nineteenth-century materialism. If you review your life experiences for magical moments that shaped your life but did not spring from the logic of materialist science, you may find many candidates for helping you believe in the miraculous.

If you act on the advice of the White Queen to Alice to believe at least six impossible things before breakfast, you will be getting closer to your goal: achieving an attitude that enables you to do the impossible.

If you want to maintain a logical, scientific attitude about beliefs, it is best to play the game of What If?

- *What if* you possessed the ability to see into the future? What would you want to know?
- *What if* you could sense other people's feelings and thoughts? Whose feelings and thoughts would you want to share?
- *What if* other people could sense your innermost feelings? Would you have anything to fear? With whom would you be willing to share that intimacy?
- *What if* you unconsciously exerted a psychic effect on other people to make your wishes come true? Would you be willing to take responsibility for your unconscious powers?
- *What if* you were able to fulfill your greatest potentials? What would they be?
- *What if* you were able to foresee how your life could work better? Would you take steps to make it that way?

Take your time with those six impossible things to believe. There will be time for many breakfasts and many more impossible things.

Exercises

Examining your beliefs
1. If you believe that seeing into the future is possible, on what do you base your belief?
2. If you are skeptical about precognition, what would it take to make you believe it?
3. Have you personally ever experienced precognition? A dream? An intuition or hunch? A gut feeling that turned out right? A psychic impression? If you have had such experience, take a moment to reexperience how you felt when your presentment came true. If it was a satisfying feeling, you are primed for precognition. If it was a scary or terrifying feeling, you will need

to work on retraining your attitude toward precognition.

4. Has anyone ever predicted anything for you that later happened? Recall your feeling when the predicted event came to pass. If you experienced panic or shock, you will need to change your attitude to a positive one. If you felt that your life was on track—being where you were supposed to be at the right time—you will feel comfortable in pursuing further adventures in precognition.

5. Has anyone ever predicted anything for you that did not happen, but you hoped it would, and were disappointed when it did not? Could the person have picked up a fantasy of yours and given it back to you as a prediction? If you are willing to admit that wrong predictions do not make right predictions impossible, you will have a good attitude for further positive experience.

6. Can you recall an experience of *déjà vu*? Was there any accompanying idea that you had dreamed of the experience before it happened? Did your *déjà vu* experience give you any belief in your personal power of precognition? If you are willing to acknowledge that it might be connected with precognition, you will have the right attitude for further exploration.

7. Have you ever experienced a series of fortuitous coincidences or a streak of good luck? How did you explain it? Did it affect your belief in the impossible? Do you take any responsibility for it?

8. Have you ever suffered through a streak of bad luck that seemed out of your control? Do you feel any responsibility for this bad luck? Do you now think that your attitude could have been a factor? If you are willing to consider the possibility that unconsciously you brought on your own bad luck, you are taking an important step toward the realization of your mind's powers.

9. What proof would it take to convince you that you personally have the ability to see into the future? Reconsider this question after you finish this book.

A Simple ESP Test: 'What was in the Microwave?'
This simple test can be played as a game with adults or children. My children love it, and usually do very well.

1. One person plays the role of experimenter and selects pairs of

household objects that are different from each other, say, a banana and a salt shaker, or an orange and a pencil. The experimenter assembles the objects in the kitchen and makes certain that the people to be tested (the subjects) do not see the objects.

2. The subjects go to the living room or some other room not adjacent to the kitchen. They have paper and pens.

3. The experimenter flips a coin to determine which of two paired objects will be the target. He puts the target in the microwave or oven or some place known to the subjects.

4. The experimenter goes to the subjects and tells them; 'Pretend that you are going out of your body and go into the kitchen and look to see what is in the microwave. You will see a picture in your mind of the target object. Draw what you see.'

5. The subjects make drawings of their mental perceptions.

6. After the drawings are finished, the experimenter goes to the kitchen and takes out the target object from the microwave. He also takes in the other hand the control object of the pair. He goes to the subjects and holds up the objects, one in each hand. 'What was in the microwave?' he asks.

7. Subjects compare their drawings with the objects and make a guess at which object was the target.

8. After the subjects have all made their guesses, the experimenter reveals which object was the actual target. The subjects examine any correspondences with their drawings. Somebody might have done a perfect drawing of the wrong object! That is called *displacement* and means that the person has good ESP ability but for some reason is unable to direct it properly.

9. If you are doing this experiment as a game, let everyone take turns at being the experimenter.

2.

Training your Dream Tigers

When we go to sleep at night and dream, the corridors of our minds are stalked by what I call *dream tigers*, our personal guardians of safety. When a dream tiger scents the approach of danger, he sends us a terrifying dream premonition that wakes us so that we can sound the alarm or flee the approaching menace. Evolved millions of years ago, before language, the dream tiger speaks in symbols and pictures. But the fierce, highly intelligent dream tiger can be trained to speak in English.

If you pay no attention to your dream tiger—if you make no effort to remember and understand your dreams—the frustrated dream tiger will savage you with unwanted and terrifying dream premonitions to get your attention. The incredible power of this remarkable beast and how it can be trained was revealed in a dream as I was beginning a study of precognitive dreams:

> *The Dream Tiger*
> I was in a cave, swimming about in a shallow pool, when a powerful Tarzan-like man appeared with a tiger. I was very frightened of the tiger, but I tried not to let on. The man was bragging a bit about the prowess of his tiger and how well trained it was. He pointed out a large pool outside the cave but very far down the mountain side. He said he would order his tiger to dive into that distant pool and return. That seemed to be an incredible feat but the tiger did it. When the tiger returned it had to pass over me, which frightened me even more. But I worked up courage and said, 'That's very good.' I was astonished when the tiger replied, 'Thank you.'
>
> 'My God,' I thought, 'it can speak English.' And I was no longer afraid of the tiger, but admired it the more.

The dream's symbolism suggests that the shallow pool in the cave is the most accessible part of our unconscious, but the Tarzan figure—the strong, primitive aspect of our inner self—can train the dream tiger to dive into a deeper part of the unconscious where the future can be glimpsed. Further, the tiger can render this precognitive information in our own language so that we can understand it and make use of it more easily. Once tamed, the dream tiger deserves our admiration.

According to my theory, our dream tigers stem from mankind's early evolutionary development. When our earliest ancestors lived in the jungles, there was constant danger from predators, especially at night when they were sleeping. But during the dreaming state, about every 90 minutes, each one's dream tiger would scan the environment for danger. When a predator, perhaps a saber-toothed tiger, approached, the dream tiger would sound the alarm by sending a premonitory dream terrifying enough to wake the adult sleeper; babies and small children, who were most vulnerable, would cry out in their sleep and wake their parents. Alarmed by this inner sentry, our ancestor would scamper to safety. Those who paid no attention to their dreams tended to be eaten; we, as survivors, inherit the primitive dream tigers, which terrify us but wish only to protect us.

So when a child awakens or cries out in terror of the night, don't say, 'It's only a dream. Go back to sleep.' Tell your child we all have special monsters—dream tigers—for protection and guidance. Encourage your child to make friends with his or her dream monster, to find out what it wants, and to ask it how the dream monster can help. Children seem unduly fascinated with monsters, and will want them as special friends.

If you have experienced a dream premonition, comfort yourself with the knowledge that you have a powerful but potentially friendly ally within yourself that can be trained to protect and guide you. The first step in making friends with your dream tiger is to learn to interpret its language—symbols. Since the dream tiger has a propensity to scan the future, your task is to convince it that you need positive, guiding information from the future. The more you communicate with your dream tiger, by recording, analyzing and interpreting dreams, the better it can serve you.

Sometimes premonitions can serve us too, but now we live in houses and have police for protection, so we usually no longer need the mighty vigilence of our dream tigers against the threat of danger. Now we can ask our tigers for dreams of *promise* instead of *premonition*.

Dream tigers, like the tigers of the jungle, can never be

completely tamed. Although with proper inducements they can be trained up to a point, they always retain the independent and fierce ways of the primal beast. Bear in mind that dreams cannot be *controlled*, merely *influenced*. Even the best-trained dream tiger will sometimes ignore your request or assert itself in unexpected ways. That's what makes them so fascinating.

Over the years I have taken more than a thousand people into meditation to discover their personal dream animal. Nearly everyone reports seeing one. The dream beasts include bears, eagles, horses, panthers, lions and even snakes. Our strong connection to special dream animals may be an inheritance from our ancient shamanic ancestors, who identified with an animal totem as their protector.

Remembering Dreams

If you have difficulty in remembering dreams, here are some hints for better dream recall:

1. Before you go to sleep at night, give yourself the suggestion that you will wake early in the morning with the memory of a dream and be able to write it.
2. Keep a pad and pen under your pillow or nearby so that when you awaken you can jot down notes. You can substitute a tape recorder if your speaking will not awaken someone else in the bedroom.
3. The last part of the dream is usually the first remembered. Work your way back to the beginning of the dream by asking, 'What came before that?'
4. You may wish to set your alarm a half hour earlier so that it will be more likely to waken you during a dream and you will have time to record it before doing anything else.
5. If you 'never' remember dreams, ask a friend (or hire someone) to sit at your bedside all night, with a dim light on, so that when your eyes are moving back and forth (rapid eye movements) your friend can wake you and ask for a report of your dream, which the friend can write down. The longest dreams come in the morning, so that is the best time for waking for dream reports.
6. If your persistent efforts do not work, you may be trying too hard. Relax and let your dreams do the work. If all else fails, try the 'artificial dreaming' techniques described in Chapter 5,

which I invented specially for people who cannot remember dreams. Some people substitute a rich waking fantasy life for nocturnal dreams, so you may be able to work with daydreams or creative fantasy.

7. When you write out your dreams, give them titles, as if they were stories. It helps to focus on the point of your dreams and may aid you in associating with the symbols and the metaphorical situations of your dreams.

Experiments in Dream Prophecy

Is there any actual scientific proof that a person can dream about the future at will? Two remarkable experimental studies done at the Maimonides Dream Laboratory in Brooklyn established conclusively that their subject, a young Englishman named Malcolm Bessent, was able to foresee randomly created events of the next day more than 60 per cent of the time.[6]

In the first Bessant study, the targets about which he was to dream were multi-sensory experiences built around a randomly chosen picture and word. For instance, when the randomly chosen words were 'parka hood', a picture of an Eskimo wearing a parka hood was chosen, Bessent was led into a room covered with white sheets to represent the Arctic, he listened to *Finlandia* by Sibelius, and had ice put down his back.

The night before the targets were chosen, Bessent dreamed of standing in a room 'surrounded by white, talking to a black man with gray-white hair' (like the Eskimo), and 'ice blue and white'. Three independent judges, who did not know which targets went with which dreams, ranked five out of eight attempts as direct hits (62.5 per cent hits, where 12.5 per cent is expected by chance), giving odds against chance of 5,000 to 1. That means that the experiment would have to be repeated 5,000 times before Bessent might be expected to dream about the future just by chance.

The second Bessent study conformed to more usual parapsychological methods by using randomly selected thematic slide shows as targets. The slide shows were randomly chosen after Bessent's dreams were recorded, by someone who did not know what the dreams were. Again there were five direct hits out of eight attempts.

The Bessent studies proved dream prophecy so conclusively that no more dream studies were ever done to prove precognition. The point had been made.

Many different subjects from all walks of life, both with and without prior psychic experience, tried 'one night stands' at psychic dreaming at the Maimonides Dream Laboratory. Out of 148 such attempts, 111, or 75 per cent, were successful. This suggests that the ability to dream psychically is widespread. When I polled the staff of the dream lab with a 300-word adjective checklist, four of us agreed on these key descriptors for good psychic dreaming subjects: *adaptable*, *adventurous*, *alert*, *appreciative*, *curious*, *enthusiastic*, *imaginative*, *individualistic*, *sensitive*, *suggestible* and *having varied interests*. Three of us agreed on *independent*, *insightful*, *original*, *relaxed*, *resourceful*, *spontaneous*, *uninhibited* and *warm*.

To describe poor subjects, we agreed on only one word: *apathetic*. Three of us agreed that poor subjects were *aloof*, *anxious*, *argumentative*, *conservative*, *conventional*, *despondent*, *nervous* and *tense*. If you think you are better described by the adjectives for the good subjects rather than those for the bad subjects, you will probably have success at training your dream tiger.

Dream Symbols

During the two years I worked as a dream subject at the Maimonides Dream Laboratory I found myself getting enormous experience at dream interpretation. By comparing my dreams with target pictures used in telepathy experiments, I was able to see how dreams symbolize and distort literal elements. The thing to look for is a basic thematic statement, for which each person might have an individual metaphor. In preparation for writing up the lab's 10 years of research material for the book *Dream Telepathy*, I reviewed literally thousands of dreams, looking for symbolic correspondences to pictures and life situations. Because independent judges had already blindly judged correspondences between dreams and targets, it became easy to see what guided their judgement. Contrary to what some physiological dream researchers say, there really *are* meaningful symbols in our dreams and they can be objectively identified. In my estimation, the 10-year body of the Maimonides psychic dream work offers the best scientific evidence that our dream symbols correspond to an external reality.

One way to sharpen your intuitive understanding of symbolic meanings would be to read the book *Dream Telepathy*, which relates hundreds of event-dream symbol correspondences. These correspondences are not derived from anyone's theory but represent the work of many judges objectively trying to match many people's dreams with many target pictures. Contrary to Sigmund Freud's assertion that dream symbols are a deliberate concealment of the dream's real content by the unconscious mind, the dream telepathy work suggests that symbols are a universal language of dreams and are easily translated once the basic principles are grasped. Our dream tigers spring from an era millions of years ago when symbols were the only tools of communication. Symbols still retain their great impact and emotional power.

Although dream symbols show a universal ability to communicate basic themes, their specific meaning for us as individuals can be highly complex and often rich in double meanings: our individual dream symbols are derived from our personal experiences and attitudes. The context in which they appear can also alter their meaning, as with words, which are also symbols. If you have any dream books that purport to tell you specific meanings for dream symbols, throw them out and start compiling your own personal symbol lexicon. Your dream tiger wants to be appreciated as an individual, with idiosyncratic symbols that can best be appreciated by *you*.

Of my several dream researcher friends, the most experienced at analyzing dream symbols is Patricia Garfield, who has recorded more than 13,000 dreams since she was a teenager. She may hold a world record for the number of recorded dreams. Author of the popular book *Creative Dreaming*, Dr Garfield displays an uncanny knack of getting to the heart of a person's dream image by asking just a few questions, such as 'Does that remind you of anything going on in your life just now?' or 'What are your feelings about that image or symbol?'

Our colleague in a dream group, Dr Gayle Delaney, proposed a method of questioning that even the most inexperienced dream interpreter could use for starters. She asks, 'If I were from a different planet, how would you define that dream image or symbol? Who or what is it? What is your attitude toward it? Assume I never heard of it, and explain everything.' She would then elicit a complete description of the dream person or symbol from the dreamer's point of view. It became obvious that the subject's dream tiger was using that symbol as shorthand to represent several things simultaneously, and often at different levels of meaning. (For extensive examples see Gayle Delaney's book *Living Your Dreams*.[7])

Our dream group would take up to two hours just to analyze one dream thoroughly, with six people working on it. We often found that our varying approaches meshed to produce a multi-tiered structure of dream meanings. We worked at it until the dreamer said, 'Aha! Now I know what it means.' That click of recognition of your dream tiger's message comes in a creative uprush of intuitive *knowing*.

Here is a dream of mine our group worked on in February 1978, when I was working on my last book, *Incredible Coincidence*, and having difficulty finding the right tone and point of view:

The Prisoner
I was being held prisoner with a group of people in a building. We were watched, but I managed to squeeze through a small doorway to freedom—an office where I found an important book. Outside there was confusion and rioting. I was given a ticket by a policeman for being naked. I complained that I had just gotten free from a kidnapping, and the police went in search of the kidnappers. Yet somehow I wound up again in the prison.

My analysis was: is this symbolic of my imprisoning my thoughts on the book to conform to peer pressure? Being naked when outside the prison might symbolize freedom of my own thought, baring my soul. I may get some censure (a ticket) but it's better than being back in prison.

When Patricia Garfield's husband Zal asked me, 'Who are the villains?' I suddenly realized that the villains, or kidnappers, were not my colleagues, but rather the skeptics. It was the skeptics who would censure me and keep me a prisoner of my own timidity, my own attempts to conform to their point of view. I resolved to find that doorway to freedom and my office where I could write that important book. I should not write books for skeptics because they don't read books that disagree with their point of view. I freed myself from that self-imposed prison, and bared my naked feelings about what I really thought. My dream tiger's message got through to me.

Call the Dream Tiger

One evening I asked Dr Garfield if, in the course of recording and analyzing 13,000 dreams, she had encountered any that seemed precognitive. Only very trivial ones, she said. I told the group of my experiences in future dreaming and emphasized the role played by our conscious will in calling up a precognitive dream. Even just becoming intrigued by the topic tends to call on the dream tiger.

A few weeks later Garfield told me of a major precognitive dream. Although she didn't realize it at the time, the dream not only answered her question about someone but also told her where he would move in the future. The situation was this: Garfield had lost contact with her Chinese meditation teacher, Mr K, who lived in the North Beach area of San Francisco but was always difficult to find. She felt an urgent need to ask him for help in her meditation techniques, but could not locate him at the regular meeting place. His students didn't know where he was either. The next time she stopped at the meeting place, it was closed.

Then the Garfields went to Hawaii for a vacation, but Patricia was still wondering how to contact the elusive Mr K. She had a dream in which he telephoned to say he was around the corner from where the Garfields lived, near the tennis courts. Could he visit her? Garfield noted that the dream telephone voice seemed 'warbly' and very emotional. But she dismissed the dream as wish fulfillment.

When she returned to San Francisco, she attempted once again to make contact with Mr K. Eventually, she heard that he had moved to her own neighbourhood, many miles from North Beach. The first clue came when the Garfields' maid recognized him at a nearby bus stop. That confirmed he was in the area.

A few days later, driving home from the doctor's office, Garfield acted on an impulse to drive by the bus stop in search of Mr K. There he was, munching on an apple. He had moved to the very next block, next to the tennis courts—as in her dream. With her new neighbour Garfield studied intensively the meditation techniques she describes in her book *Pathway to Ecstasy: The Dream Mandala*.

Patricia Garfield's dream tiger not only answered her question with psychic information but signaled that an important relationship was about to develop. A clue to the dream's psychic origin was the 'warbly' voice on the telephone, since psychic dreams about others often contain images of unusual communication. Once the topic of precognitive dreaming was brought up, Garfield's dream tiger delivered the psychic goods in a straightforward description of where Mr K would move. It will be interesting to see if more of Garfield's dreams contain psychic information now that her dream tiger has demonstrated its prowess at future consciousness.

At one of my seminars in Chicago, my students called up their dream tigers to search for a lion. Before the final day of the seminar, I gave the group some examples of dream precognition and told them they had a nocturnal homework assignment: dream about what would happen to them the next morning. I gave them the suggestion that they would have a vivid dream about the future experience and would be able to remember it and write it down. I had no idea what we would be doing the next morning; I had only the plan to build a target experience around whatever symbol should appear in my own dream the next morning. I dreamed of someone riding a lion around a fountain and being chased by others. Locating a book with a picture of a lion, I returned to the seminar room now armed with a plan.

All the students but one had remembered and recorded dreams, which we filed away until later. The young man who had no dream received as punishment the role of the lion. We used chairs to construct a fountainlike circle in the middle of the room, a young woman volunteered to ride our 'lion', and the rest of us gave noisy chase around the 'fountain'. It was a good excuse to act like kids again, and we all enjoyed our rousing chase around the fountain where we paused to look at the picture of the lion. Our two-footed lion was becoming weary from his four-footed flight, so we called an end to our target experience and the students went to retrieve their dreams.

Remarkably, all the students who reported dreams had in fact dreamed about some aspect of the morning's experience, each from their own point of view, interests, and concerns. No one dreamed about a lion, but instead they had dreamed about the human interaction that took place, provoked by my dream about a lion. The group agreed the experiment was a smashing success; it showed them that they could call upon their dream tiger at will.

Guiding Dreams

What we often need from our dreams is guidance about our present situation, help in solving the problem that confronts us right now. Then it's time to call the dream tiger for a guiding dream.

In January 1978 I was lamenting that my efforts at writing *Incredible Coincidence* did not seem to be jelling. My research, which involved collecting stories of coincidence over the years, was completed, but as my agent remarked when I showed him a draft of a couple of chapters, the material seemed to lack organization. I fretted about this for months. Finally, I called on my dream tiger for guidance.

I dreamed that I was looking at Carl Jung's book entitled *Synchronicity* (meaningful coincidence). The chapters were short, with long titles written in script. The chapters were subdivided into cases, which were numbered in Roman numerals. I saw the opening page of a chapter printed as 'The Search for Eliot Carter, Case *xxi*,' and centered on the page. The whole effect was quite aesthetic. I wondered if it were an idea for *my* book on synchronicity.

I had seen Jung's book *Synchronicity*, a recent trade paperback, but had not bought it since I had his original essay. But the dream prompted me to purchase it and to note that it bore a Roman numeral series number, *xx*, of the Bollingen Series. My book would follow it, symbolically, becoming *xxi*. Until this dream I had not considered using cases, case titles and case numbers. But when I tried writing the book that way, it began to flow and felt right.

Taking the dream's advice, I actually did title a chapter 'The Search for Eliot Carter'. Significantly, that chapter deals with writers making use of coincidence and psychic sensing to find the material they need for their books. My dream tiger provided both literal and symbolic guidance, nicely printed out in English.

In January 1981 my problem pattern asserted itself once more: How to do the book at hand? As before, I had been fretting for several months and was becoming increasingly dissatisfied with my outline. The writing was not flowing. I knew this meant that something was wrong in the book's organization and viewpoint. But what? And what to do about it? The deadline for the manuscript's submission had already passed, so I issued an emergency call for the dream tiger. I dictated suggestions into my tape recorder and played them back before I went to sleep:

> Recall the last time you conquered a similar situation. How did you feel? (I felt excited, enthusiastic, inspired.) That was the last time I had a guiding dream. I need a guiding dream now. I need a dream that will inspire me, excite me, make me enthusiastic, and give me the plan. If it is not the right time to do this, I must know that too. I need to hear from my dream tiger. Expect a dream early in the morning and record it—no matter what the dream is.

That night I awoke several times with dreams but strangely, when

I arose early in the morning to write them down, I forgot them. I was about to reproach myself for this, when suddenly a single thought trumpeted through my mind: '*Build the book around how-to examples.*' My dream tiger was communicating directly in plain English. There was no need to analyze dream symbols. I knew exactly what to do.

The emotion accompanying this simple sentence was euphoric; it carried the excitement, enthusiasm and inspiration that I had requested.

Admittedly, I had hoped the dream tiger would pay me a visit long before this, but I had not formally issued an invitation. Dream tigers are sensitive and do not like to be taken for granted.

Although we all want to hear that our ideas and aspirations are brilliantly inspired and will lead to certain success, it is better to get a no from our dream tiger than to find life giving you a no. Once I conceived what I thought was a clever and brilliant idea—producing a television show about fake psychic demonstrations, done by magicians and called 'the All-American Fake Psychic Show'. I fantasized details of this before going to bed, and requested a visit from my dream tiger to show me how best to accomplish this. In the morning I awoke with a dream of biting on thistles—thorns were penetrating my tongue and cheeks. That seemed to be my dream tiger's 'tongue in cheek', humorous way of telling me *no*. I dropped the idea immediately.

Guiding dreams often displace the necessary action onto someone else in a symbolic way. For instance, a young woman told me of a dream in which her former boyfriend was trying to telephone her. She wondered if the dream might be precognitive of his calling her in the future. I suggested that her dream meant that *she* wanted to establish communication with the former boyfriend—after all, it was *her* dream. Either she could wait by the telephone for the next few years, or she could take the dream tiger's advice and telephone the boyfriend herself. Be alert to possible advice for yourself when your dream image shows someone else taking the action.

Training your Dream Tiger

Training dream tigers is not unlike training real tigers: a tiger trainer approaches the animal with great respect, knowing that it can never be tamed completely but will retain its ways of the wild. The trainer establishes communication with the tiger, shows it time and time again what he wants it to do and always rewards it when the desired feat is performed. So-called 'affection training' relies on rewarding the animal with treats when it does what you want it to. No whips, no threats, no abuse are permitted. The idea is to establish a rapport between the trainer and the tiger so that the highly intelligent animal will perform his magnificent feats out of friendship and respect.

In the 20 years since my dream tiger first appeared, I have noticed a subtle change in my dreams. Since I began recording and interpreting my dreams, there have been fewer and fewer images of violence, terror or other negative events. This change was an unsought by-product of my intellectual attempt to generate precognitive dreams.

My two basic questions were: Is it possible to determine before-hand which dreams might be precognitive? And is it possible to actually program dreams to reveal the future? Since my initial interest was mainly theoretical, I wondered if there were any limits to precognition. Could I dream about an event the next day as easily as about one 10 years in the future? To answer those ques-tions, I had to record my dreams and pay close attention to them to determine whether they might be ordinary or precognitive.

Some dreams seemed symbolic, others realistic, and some were mixed. To understand them fully I had to probe into the symbolism of my dreams. I began to make predictions about which dreams might eventually prove precognitive. And when they were fulfilled I rejoiced and entered an eager note in my dream journal. What I did not realize until recently was that this very process—giving positive feedback to my unconscious—was training the dream tiger. I was not only communicating with it, I was rewarding it with my enthusiasm when it did what I wanted it to: dream about the future. Unwittingly, I was giving my dream tiger affection training and being rewarded in turn with more dreams of promise and fewer premonitions.

Unlike others who have experienced the terror or premonitions, I now look forward to my dreams. When my dreams predict the future, they nearly always give me images of promise and instill faith that the future is worth the present struggle.

I suspect that the true therapeutic effect of psychoanalysis and other mind-healing systems that use dream interpretation as their basis derives from helping you communicate with your dreams and dream tigers.

One such communication came in a long, bizarre dream of

28 April 1974, in which I had a vision of 'the land of the living dead'. At one point, I came to a stage where a man was acting as a judge interviewing a woman. It was as if they had done the scene many times. *Someone accompanied them on a blue piano.*

More than two years later, on 5 September 1976, I visited the Renaissance Faire near San Francisco and, amidst the weird goings-on, I was astonished to see someone playing a blue piano, accompanying a stage performance of the Monteverdi opera *Incoronazione di Poppea*, the story of Nero's wife, the evil empress of Rome. Never before or since have I seen anyone playing a blue piano, much less one accompanying a stage performance. This correspondence was odd enough to make me consider the complete dream again and ponder it.

The Land of the Living Dead

Two others and I were exploring an ancient underground sewer in Europe when we found some valuable objects from the eighteenth century. But we doubted that the local merchants would realize their worth.

We began excavating and found an ancient stone pavement on which were coloured pictures, which together made up a story. Then someone came in with a document from a scholar, a document which independently told of the significance of the story in stone. We saw that there were six graves nearby; the bodies began to come to life. It seemed that the marvelous story in stone had somehow kept them alive.

The scene then cut to a later time. Now there were many caverns hollowed out. I was sent to inspect one. Each of them was crowded with 'the living dead' who went through various routines of life, but automatically. They had somehow been resuscitated by the magic stone. In one cavern there were weird sights as in a Fellini movie. Strange animals were kept in pens. Water lapped at the edges of the cavern. I came to a stage where a man was acting as a judge interviewing a woman. She had a list of how many times she had done penance, and when the judge asked her how many times, she replied, 'Oh, you know perfectly well,' as if they had done the scene many times. Someone accompanied them on a blue piano.

In the next cavern many people were lined up, going forward, like slaves chained to each other, endlessly repeating the same action.

Then suddenly, I was above ground. Walking along, I found some money on the ground. A young boy said it was his and that he really needed it. So I gave him the money and accompanied him to the store where he bought food. I told him of the land of the living dead.

My associations to the dream included: 'I think of the scene in Fellini's *Roma* where a group discover an ancient Roman villa underground; also of the *Satyricon*, in which the boys visit a brothel where each woman had a pen in a cavern. The story in stone reminds me of an ancient mosaic of Alexander the Great.'

Symbolically, the land of the living dead might represent the acting out of ancient archetypes of behaviour patterns without understanding their origin. The ancient story in stone with magical properties could represent the symbols of the collective unconscious that activate the archetypes. Most people, like the merchants, do not understand the real value of these ancient things. Yet people, like the boy, must live in practical ways that require money for food. They too should know of the land of the living dead.

The dream suggests that sometimes we compulsively act out the same patterns of life, over and over again, like neurotic zombies. We, like the boys in the decadent Rome of the *Satyricon*, are driven by the ancient archetypes to reenact the same life stories without realizing their ancient origin. We get stuck in a very old rut. But by understanding *why* we do these same destructive things again and again, we can break out of that rut and emerge above ground where we can find real nourishment for our inner selves. By knowing of the land of the living dead, we can free ourselves from it. Rather than acting out the ancient archetypes of the collective unconscious, we must find out from our inner selves the guiding images meant specifically for us, in order to achieve any personal fulfillment.

My dream tiger emphasized this message by provocatively previsioning an opera about the decadent ways of ancient Rome, with the absurd touch of a blue piano accompanying.

The most useful feat that our dream tigers can perform for us is to show us glimpses of our blueprint of life locked in the inner self. By discovering these guiding images—blueprints of our secret destiny—we make the first step toward fulfilling them. To learn the language of our dream tigers, we must practice with our own dreams. When some measure of dream mastery is achieved, then we know that our dream tigers are becoming trained and will perform marvelous feats for us.

Exercises

Programming Your Dream Tiger

1. Write down an important question in your life right now, or some problem that faces you. For example, you may need to make a major decision or need some information from the future that might affect your decision. You want to know how your decision will affect your future.

2. Write out or dictate on your tape recorder the following instructions for playback or reviewing just before you go to bed:

> I need advice and guidance from my dream tiger. I need a dream that will answer my question: [read your question]. I want my dream tiger to give me the answer in simple terms that I can understand. I will arise early in the morning with the dream answer fresh in my mind. I shall be able to remember it easily and write it down. Its meaning will become clear to me. I shall follow the advice of my dream tiger.

3. In the morning record your dreams. If no dreams are recalled, try again for two more nights. If you still have no success, review the section earlier in this chapter, 'Remembering Dreams'. Write down your associations with the main dream images and symbols. It may help to define, as if for someone else, what the images are.

4. If the dream is complicated, restate it as a basic theme or short story, ignoring for the moment the details.

5. What emotions accompanied the dream? Close your eyes and re-experience the dream and pay close attention to the accompanying emotions.

6. If your question could be answered with a yes or no, determine if the dream story and the emotions are positive or negative as an answer.

7. If your question is more complicated, as in asking for information about the future, consider the basic tone and feelings. Does the presumed future event of the dream seem rewarding? If so, act in such a way as to fulfill that prediction. If your predicted event is negative in tone, make the decision to avoid that future.

8. If your dream does indeed reveal an answer, give you inspiration, or some guiding image from the inner self, keep your promise with the dream tiger. Act on it!

3.

Experiments in Time

Our major scientific publications do not publish *experiments in time*, seeing into the future. The prestigious journal *Science* and its more popular sister, *Scientific American*, sometimes attack parapsychology, but they do not publish the experimental facts they attack. And so, predictably, the vast majority of scientists have no knowledge of the experimental literature of precognition.

Methods used by the science establishment to suppress research into parapsychology and allied mind disciplines were recently summarized by Senator Claiborne Pell, a Democrat from Rhode Island, in *Omni*[8].

> One way to avoid unpopular topics is to manipulate the university curriculum by keeping controversial subjects out of the classroom. This serves to suppress knowledge and potential interest in the subject Ridicule is also used to intimidate a scientist from daring to conduct research in unpopular fields. The most powerful suppression, however, is administered by professional journals that refuse to accept reports in nontraditional areas, such as research exploring the depths of human consciousness. This censorship severely reduces the opportunity to build interest and potential insight into the various avenues of interdisciplinary research.

That is worse than a pity. It is a crippling deficiency in scientific understanding of how the universe works—especially that most mysterious part of the universe: the human mind.

'Extraordinary claims demand extraordinary proof,' goes the conventional scientific wisdom often quoted by astronomer Carl Sagan. In his best-selling book and television series, *Cosmos*, the universe works quite nicely without precognition. Sagan's cosmos may have conjectural entities like black holes but it does not deal with the hard data of precognition. Pooh-poohing astrological newspaper horoscopes, as Sagan does, cannot come close to achieving scientific scrutiny of the human ability to see into the future. Precognition must be ignored or disposed of by intellectual arrogance if the dominant ways of picturing the universe are to be safely held in the vaults of science. But those vaults are cracking at the seams. The cracks gape wider every time a new experiment in time shows that we can see into the future.

To provide that extraordinary proof of my extraordinary claim of precognition, let us look at a number of experiments whose odds against chance could not be explained away in a million years—or a far greater period of time in our first case.

The Proof

My nomination for the most convincing scientific proof of precognition goes to Dr Richard C. Neville, a professor of electrical engineering at Northern Arizona University in Flagstaff. In 1975, when Neville was teaching at the University of California at Santa Barbara, he presented a paper to the parapsychological Association convention in which his subject achieved odds against chance for precognition of 1,000,000,000,000,000,000,000,000,000,000,000, 000,000,000,000,000,000,000,000,000,000,000 to one, that is, 10 to the 66th power! It would take several times longer than the universe has been in existence (10 to 20 billion years) of doing such experiments before the results could be attributed to chance.

Neville's experiment could not have been simpler. It required no special apparatus, not even a famous psychic, since his subject was a student who remains anonymous. The experiment is one you have probably tried yourself on a modest level: predicting which one of two elevators will come first.[9]

In preliminary experiments with ESP cards, Neville's subject showed great success at clairvoyance (guessing targets no human knows) but scored only at chance level when he tried precognition. Neville thought better results might come with something that the subject could get more involved in, such as the elevators in the engineering building. From 1971 to 1974, a total of 42 months, they agreed to conduct elevator-calling experiments. Neville carefully counted the number of times each elevator came first so that he could make sure that their arrivals were indeed random. If both elevators arrived at the same time, the trial was aborted. In total the subject guessed 2,807 times which elevator would come first. He was right 67 per cent of the time. We know that sensory cues were ruled out effectively because Neville's subject achieved his highest scoring rate (77 per cent) when he made his guesses at home by telephone 16 hours before the target times.

Over so many trials the limits of chance ran out as Neville showed that only some paranormal process could account for this incredible departure from chance.

My next contender in the precognition odds-against-chance hall of fame is Dr Helmut Schmidt, a physicist now at Mind Science Foundation in San Antonio, Texas. Schmidt's subjects racked up odds against chance of a billion to one in 60,000 trials of guessing which of four lights would be lit by a random quantum process (decay of radioactive strontium 90). Schmidt screened a hundred subjects before he found his psychic stars: a housewife, a truck driver and a medium.

Honorary mention goes to the pioneer researcher of precognition, Dr J.B. Rhine. In research in the 1930s at Duke University, odds of three million to one were achieved by several subjects who predicted the turn of ESP cards.[10]

To produce scientific proof of a phenomenon, several criteria must be applied. First, a proper scientific experiment must be performed and the results scrutinized by peers for presentation at an official meeting of a scientific society or for publication in a journal. The experiment must be replicated, preferably by another researcher at another laboratory. The experiments must be statistically significant—that is, odds against chance must be at least 20 to 1 (probability or $p<.05$). And, in the case of controversial experiments such as those of parapsychology, fraud must be ruled out. The best way of doing that is not depending on any one experimenter or subject but having many experiments done at many laboratories by many researchers with many subjects.

How many experiments showing proof of precognition have been published? Going through the authoritative series, *Research in Parapsychology* (see note at the beginning of the Sources), published annually as the official proceedings of the convention of the international Parapsychological Association—affiliated with the American Association for the Advancement of Science—I stopped counting after reaching 60 experiments. Going through the parapsychological journals from 1937–80, another researcher found 32 major studies showing statistically significant proof of precognition.[11] All the criteria have been demonstrated beyond doubt—certainly beyond any proof offered by conventional psychology for any of its major findings.

When we know that precognition does work, the big scientific question becomes. '*How* does precognition work? And how does it affect other sciences?

But it is the human question that is most interesting. What can these experiments in time show us about the best way to use our latent precognitive abilities? What are the optimum conditions for seeing into the future? What mental strategies should we take when attempting prevision? What clues can be found to tell us how best to use precognition in our own lives?

The Human Use of Precognition

The first thing we learned from five decades of experiments in precognition is that repetitive guessing at known targets (so-called 'forced-choice' experiments) brings on a decline effect. The more you guess ESP cards, the worse you get.

Probably the most potent factor in forced-choice tests tht goes against ESP success resides in the use of the *left-brain* in guessing. Our dominant left hemisphere of the brain, which is engaged for logical, analytical tasks, predominates when we know what the answers are and are asked to select one. For psychic functioning, the right hemisphere predominates, yet the left hemisphere overrules the right when logic comes into play. So the less you know about the answer, the better you will do in using your ESP.

The information that is likely to be right when you first attempt to see into the future includes shapes, contours, visual images, colors, textures, feelings and emotions. That type of material comes mainly from the right brain. The information that is likely to be wrong includes names, numbers, addresses, dates and anything you *guess* at. That is analytical information from the left hemisphere, which must be trained to be psychic. For that reason, researchers tell their untrained subjects: 'Tell us what you *see*, not what you *think*. Don't make any guesses.'

Successful techniques for eliciting psychic information from subjects in their ordinary waking consciousness were developed by physicist Harold Puthoff and Russell Targ at Stanford Research Institute (now SRI International) in Menlo Park, California. In a long series of 'remote viewing' experiments, they showed that with over one hundred subjects, two-thirds were able to successfully activate their psychic ability to describe unknown locations at a distance. Since they did only one experiment a day, there was no decline effect.[12] A dozen other laboratories tried their techniques with subjects who had no previous psychic experience, and again found great success in eliciting psychic information in remote viewing experiments. Not everyone who tried these experiments got results, however, for reasons we shall consider in the next section.

The next step for the SRI researchers was to demonstrate precognitive remote viewing. They used the same experimental protocol as before, but the targets were randomly chosen *after* the subject made a description of the unknown location where the outbound experimenter would be. The first subject in precognitive remote viewing was a professional photographer, Hella Hammid, who initially came into the psychic program as a control subject. She was stunned when her first attempts at psychic sensing proved extraordinarily accurate and precise.[13] She now does work as a professional psychic consultant for the Mobius Society in Los Angeles.

In 1975 Hella Hammid tried four times to see into the future. Independent blind judges gave her four direct hits—a 100 per cent accuracy rate. Who knows? Perhaps on your first attempt at precognitive remote viewing you may do as well. Here is what Hammid described before outbound experimenter Harold Punthoff arrived on the four scenes.

1. 'Some kind of congealing tar, or maybe an area of condensed lava ... that has oozed out to fill up some kind of boundaries.' [Dr Puthoff arrived at the Palo Alto Yacht Harbor to find it filled with mud.]
2. 'A formal garden, very well manicured.' [Puthoff visited the formal garden at Stanford University Hospital.]
3. 'A black iron triangle that someone had somehow walked into.' She heard a 'squeak, squeak, about once a second.' [Puthoff went to a child's playground and amused himself on a swing shaped like a triangle. It squeaked.]
4. 'A very tall structure located among city streets covered with Tiffanylike glass.' [Puthoff visited the Palo Alto City Hall, resplendent with its glass windows.]

This information about the four target locales made the the judging very easy; anyone could tell them apart.

In fact, it seemed too easy. When a young researcher named John Bisaha, at Mundelein College in Chicago, heard about the experiment, he challenged the SRI claim that anyone could to it. A

Chicago television station asked Bisaha to arrange an informal precognitive remote viewing experiment in Chicago. To everyone's shock, it worked. It worked so well that it launched Bisaha into a new career: doing precognitive remote perception experiments. His colleague in these experiments was one of his students at the time, Brenda Dunne, who had no previous psychic experience. Dunne is now a member of the Princeton University Research Staff, where she continues to pursue her interest in this field. Bisaha now serves on the advisory board of the Midwest Parapsychological Research Institute in Chicago. So beware if you set out to challenge psychic claims by doing experiments to disprove them. You may end up as a parapsychologist!

Let's look at a couple of good examples of Dunne and Bisaha's precognitive remote perception work when the outbound experimenter, or agent (Bisaha), went 5,000 miles away to Eastern Europe and the percipient (Dunne) was asked to describe 24 hours ahead of time where he would be a prearranged time for five consecutive days. The outbound experimenter had no planned itinerary, so the percipient had no idea of the nature of locations of the eventual targets.

The first target locale was a 'flying-saucer' restaurant on the Danube River, Bratislava, Czechoslovakia. The building was circular, raised on pillars high into the air above a footbridge near the bank of the river.

The percipient foresaw the agent being 'near water ... a very large expanse of water ... boats ... vertical lines like poles ... a circular shape like a merry-go-round ... it seems to have height, maybe with poles ... a dark fence along a walk ... like a path or walkway ... a boardwalk and there's a fence along it.'

The second target was the Exhibition of Economic Achievement of the USSR, Moscow. In front there is a huge iron gate within a stone archway, ornate and carved. The agent noted that there was 'building after building inside. A Museum of Science and Industry based on a Disneyland format.'

The percipient foresaw 'a busy, urban sort of site. Busyness, movement. Different shapes and activity. Buildings ... some sort of gate or fence ... made of metal of some sort—it's high for a gate ... dark metal ... something like a doorway or a row of doorways.'

Visual images or shapes, contours, and relationships dominate this right-brained success at precognitive remote viewing. Abstract ideas, such as function (that the circular shape was a restaurant), appear less frequently, since the left, logical half of the brain commands such understanding. As we shall see later, balanced interhemispheric brain functioning—rarely achieved by anyone in our educational system—is best for integrating both analytical and intuitive information. When you first attempt precognition, do not ask *what it is*, but *what it looks like*.

Dunne and Bisaha found that their subjects scored direct hits 53.5 per cent of the time.[14] That may mean that you have at least a 50/50 chance of success in your own experiments in time.

The 'Good' versus the 'Bad' Experimenters

One of the most important findings of parapsychology—with implications for *all* experimental science—is that some personality types make good experimenters while opposite personalities make bad experimenters. Of course, the heart of experimental psychology resides in the subject-experimenter relationship. In parapsychology this relationship goes beyond physical interaction between the subjects and experimenters, and works even when the experimenter does not meet the subjects. There is much evidence that some individuals are innately incapable of carrying out a successful psychic experiment. To their frustration, a number of such individuals are parapsychologists. Although they work very hard, and really would like to prove ESP, they have been denied their wish to witness the miraculous.

A prime ingredient for psychic success in experiments is the rapport between experimenter and subject. A comfortable, intimate and warm relationship makes ESP possible. If you are able to enter into good rapport with others, you should do well at ESP testing. If you have trouble relating to other people, you will have problems. You may even be 'psi-inhibitory'.

The differences between 'psi-conductive' and 'psi-inhibitory' experimenters were brilliantly shown by New York City College psychologists Gertrude Schmeidler and Michaeleen Maher. Obtaining videotapes of 10 parapsychologists giving present-ations—five 'good' and five 'bad' experimenters—the researchers showed them to college students and asked them to rate the experimenters on a scale of five for a number of personality traits. (The sound on the tapes was turned down too low to hear, so only visual clues were present.) The good experimenters were rated as being more flexible, friendly, free, likable, warm, enthusiastic and playful. The bad experimenters were rated as being more rigid, cold, overconfident, tense, irritable, egoistic and unfriendly.[15]

Someone suggested that perhaps the good experimenters were a little too free, and might be sloppy in their experiments, so a follow-up study was done with a small group of experimenters who were considered 'careful' by their colleagues. The good, careful experimenters were rated as being more enthusiastic, active, flexible and confident. The bad, careful experimenters were considered more tense, cold, rigid, dull, irritable, egoistic and overconfident.

Of course, the researchers were measuring what other people think about the experimenters from watching them, which is important, since potential subjects would feel the same way.

When both studies are combined, the key words describing the good experimenters are: *enthusiastic* and *flexible*. The bad experimenters are seen to be *cold*, *rigid*, *overconfident* and *egoistic*.

If, in addition to being considered cold, rigid, overconfident and egoistic, you are also a skeptic, you will have an iron-clad case for the nonexistence of ESP. It will never happen for you.

The implication for the other experimental sciences is, according to my theory, that the same kind of results should hold with nonhuman subjects as well. The good experimenters, enthusiastic and flexible, will get results, whether it be from rats, tissue culture, people or nuclear particles. The bad experimenters will not be able to replicate those results, and will tend to go into other activities after being disappointed at their lack of success.

Headline Predictions

Perhaps the most common pseudoexperiment in time is predicting newspaper headlines. This is how stage performers—mentalists—do the headline-prediction illusion: a sealed envelope containing the prediction is sent to some official for safekeeping before the mentalist arrives, then after the target newspaper has been published, the envelope is opened by the mentalist, who shows everyone the exact words or nearly exact words of his prediction that matches the headline. The skill of the mentalist comes into play when he is able to switch the paper in the envelope with a paper he has just written out, after looking at the published headline. Magician Milbourne Christopher told me that he knows 40 ways of making this switch—some quite dramatic in their theatrical effect.

Beginners can purchase a trick knife that contains a chamber for concealing the headline. When the knife is inserted into the sealed envelope, which is really empty, the 'prophetic' headline is thrust into the envelope from the knife's secret chamber. A mentalist star is born.

I see no harm when such illusions are performed with the audience's knowledge that a trick is involved. But when performers misrepresent themselves as genuine psychics, they should be exposed as sleight-of-hand artists. For one thing, the ease with which these phonies perform such remarkable 'psychic' feats gives the public the idea that anyone who claims to be psychic ought to be able to do such feats. That makes it rough on those of us who do the real thing; the public has unrealistic expectations.

When you watch a performer who claims that he can predict exact headlines, look for the sealed envelope. The one way you know for sure that it cannot be a trick is if people have *read* the headline before the newspaper is made up and published. When you see performers on television, regard their feats as entertainment only.

Is it possible to predict newspaper headlines? The one way to find out is to try it. In January 1981 I did an experiment in which I attempted to predict the front page of the *Los Angeles Times*. There is no way to preset odds against chance for such real-life experiments, but I felt that if there were any correspondences with actual news stories that it would be interesting, though certainly not scientific proof of anything. My experiment, on 10 January, in which I attempted to predict the front page of 24 January, was performed under light hypnosis with the help of West Los Angeles hypnotist Kerry Gaynor. The predictions were sent to the Central Premonitions Registry.

Here is my evaluation of the experiment of 10 January:

1. *Prediction*: 'A large photograph three columns wide shows a rescue attempt of a man in a high place. He is in pain and cannot get down. A fire ladder is being sent up to him. The fire ladder is shown at an angle on the right side of the photo.'

   Correspondence: To the *Los Angeles Times* of 29 January, five days after my target date. A large photograph, three columns wide, shows 'Fire Captain Mike Reagan grimaces in pain after he and Fireman Burton E. Sander, legs tangled in ladder, fell from the facade of a North Hollywood restaurant while fighting blaze. Eight fire fighters were injured and one died when the roof collapsed. Story on page 3.'

   Another photo on page 3 shows two fire fighters on the roof and a ladder at an angle on the right side of the photo.

2. *Prediction*: 'Drug Dealer Slain....' There are more words in the headline. The story is about drugs and law enforcement. The drug dealer's death arose from an altercation involving the police trying to crack a drug ring. Cocaine is the main substance trafficked. A statement from a police lieutenant (name beginning with R, like Ryan) says police are close to cracking the drug circle because of the man's death. The investigation is going forward.

   Correspondence: To the target day, 24 January, the *Los Angeles Times* ran on page 28 a story entitled: 'Hollywood Cocain Ring Struck for Second Time by Sheriff's Deputies.' No death was involved. There is a statement by a police lieutenant whose name begins with R (Robert) who says the investigation into the ring was continuing and more arrests are expected. The story is about drugs and law enforcement. Cocaine is the main substance trafficked.

3. *Prediction*: A blizzard hitting the East Coast from New York to Maine.

   Correspondence: Southern California's largest winter storm made the front page of 29 January: 'Storm Brings Smiles, Snarls to Southland.'

From a parapsychological point of view, the correspondences with the first two predictions suggest that coincidence cannot easily account for the correct details.

Like any other skill, precognition improves with practice. Here are some tips for beginners who try the experiments in the Exercise section. First, try to sense emotions in the target, say a picture. Then look in your mind's eye at shapes and contours of objects. My fireman's ladder in the first prediction started as a pole at an angle on the right side. Only later did the information come that it was a fireman's ladder (function). After you describe the objective shapes, contours, and relationships, ask what it might mean or what the function might be.

The best psychic results come, I believe, to individuals who have trained their right and left hemispheres to work togehter. In an informal test I took of hemispheric brain functioning, my ability at balanced interhemispheric functioning was highly unusual. After that, my right brain dominated. This has not always been so. In my school days I was strongly left-brain dominated, and have only within the past 20 years trained myself to work with both halves of the brain in psychic sensing experiments.

If you have an unusual ability at balanced brain functioning, you may have extraordinary success at getting such analytical information as names (or initials), numbers, and functions in your psychic-sensing experiments. If, for instance, you are a writer or editor—someone who uses words a lot—and you also have an excellent visual sense—if you are an artist, for example, and you recall things equally well in words or pictures—you are a prime candidate for superb psychic functioning.

Such balanced brain functioning will be of greatest advantage to those who have inborn psychic talent of better than average quality. Although everyone, according to my theory, *must* be psychic, some are more gifted than others, as with all human talents. And in developing all human talents, practice counts for a lot. The greater demands for accuracy that you impose on yourself, the greater will be your achievements.

Exercises

Precognitive Remote Viewing

1. Think of a friend or acquaintance whose activities are varied but whose schedule you do not know. Pick a target time in the near future (say, 4.30 Friday afternoon) for which you will attempt to describe what your friend's activities will be at that time.
2. Sit quietly for 10 minutes and let impressions come to mind of where your friend will be, what he or she will be doing and what the surroundings are like. Make a drawing of what you see, and record your mental imagery and feelings. Do *not* attempt to *guess*; just make a record of what you see. After you have finished recording your imagery and feelings, you may then attempt to interpret their meaning.
3. After the target time has passed, telephone your friend to say you were doing an experiment in time and would like to know what he or she was doing at the target time. Convey your impressions and later show your friend your drawing. Compare notes to discover any unusual correspondences. You may find that your impressions were accurate for a different time from that of your target time.

Front-Page Prediction

1. Your target will be the front page of your local newspaper, one week from today. Tell yourself precisely what you are to do: visualize the front page of [name of paper] on [specific date].

You will see the featured photograph in your mind's eye. You will also sense a major story of that day.

2. Sit quietly for 10 minutes and conjure impressions, both visual and verbal, of what the picture shows. Make a drawing of all the details you see in your mind's eye. Now ask for an interpretation of what the picture might be, such as its basic theme. If any other impressions come, record them. Now ask for the theme of the major story and record those impressions.

3. When the target day arrives, compare the front page of your newspaper with your drawing and impressions. Also check the other stories of that day. Note any correspondences.

4. If there are no correspondences, you may want to check the newspapers for a few days afterward to see if you hit at a later time. if you found an interesting correspondence you may want to repeat this experiment and register your prediction with a friend.

4.

Making Contact

The most frustrating and paradoxical aspect of psychic functioning is that others may know our own future better than ourselves, that a psychic stranger can make contact with our inner consciousness to reveal possible futures that our logical minds have blocked off from our own self-knowledge.

Contact with Criminals

Before psychic contact can be made with others to describe their possible futures, contact of some sort must be made in the present. The most difficult type of contact to establish is with someone who doesn't want information to be known.

A case in point began as a missing person case. A 14-year-old girl was missing from her home in Lancaster, Pennsylvania. District Attorney Mick Ranck sent a photo of the girl to Stephen Schwartz of the Mobius Society and asked for any psychic information that might lead to finding her. Schwartz handed me the photo and asked where the girl was. I replied that she had been murdered. I described an assault on the girl by a man who had a history of mental problems. I described his car, said he was a teacher, and gave his specific location from the girl's house. Lancaster police began to search for the girl's body. After the body was found in a shallow grave, police were able to locate the murderer. The girl had taken karate lessons from him. He lived at the distance and in the direction I had specified. He was convicted of murder and is now serving a life sentence in a penitentiary. Commenting on the case in a *Nova* TV show on ESP in 1984, Ranck estimated that the psychic information was over 85 per cent correct. The case shows how links through another person—particularly if they are charged with emotion—can suffice to make psychic contact.

Honorable Howard E. Goldfluss, acting justice of the New York Supreme Court, recently commented in *Omni* on the increasing acceptability of psychics.[16] As evidence that psychics can provide helpful information to the police, Goldfluss cites the work of Greta Alexander of Delavon, Illinois, who helped police find two drowning victims in 1977. In a 1983 case, Alexander led a team of police through woods to a body's remains, which as she had predicted, were found near a bridge and a rock pile, with the head detached.

Goldfluss notes that defamers of psychics had better be prepared with the facts. When John D. Merrill, a founder of Northwest Skeptics, called psychic Noreen Reiner of Medford, Oregon, a fraud, she sued for libel. At the trial she testified that she instructed police trainees on the value of psychic intervention in police cases. The jury awarded Reiner 25,000 dollars.

About the use of psychics in criminal cases, Goldfluss says, 'Evidence is always a matter of degree. Loose ends prevail in the courtroom. Certainty is a rare commodity. Psychics do not solve crimes, nor do they resolve lawsuits. But if they contribute in any way to the discovery of the truth, then they can't be ignored.'

Contact with Others

In April 1974, on a visit to England, I found myself playing the role of a psychic stranger to a British television newscaster. He asked me who was going to be the next prime minister of England when the next election would be held. (There had been an election just recently.) Since I do not follow British politics, I had no logical idea. So I tuned into the newscaster—made psychic contact with him—to see the future through his unconscious.

'There will be another election within a year,' I said, 'maybe around November. I don't see either Wilson or Heath [the current party leaders] as the next prime minister. They will be replaced by a physically large person, someone with a military background.'

My prediction surprised me as much as the newscaster, but the imagery in my mind's eye was accompanied by a certain feeling in the solar plexus region that told me I was making a genuine psychic contact. I told the prediction to a writer for the London *Daily Express*, which published it on 27 April 1974.[17] In November an election was held again—it was the first time in 50 years that two elections were held the same year—and the new prime minister was James Callaghan, a former naval officer whose father was a career naval officer. His nickname is 'Big Jim'.

I know I wasn't telepathically reading the newscaster's mind for his opinions, since after the show he quizzed me with various names of possible candidates but did not mention Callaghan. I must have been tapping into his future consciousness, since a newscaster has a keen interest in political elections.

The pattern repeated seven years later, in April 1981, when a reporter from the *Daily Express* telephoned me to get my prediction about Prince Charles and his forthcoming marriage. I was about to complain that I had never met Prince Charles, when I recalled that we had been introduced in 1967, when I was visiting Cambridge University. So I did make a prediction: he will have three children—two boys and a girl—and will become Prince Regent around 1989–91. So far Charles has fulfilled two-thirds of the first prediction by having two boys.

The most dependable way of making psychic contact with another person is by being in his or her presence and touching the subject, as palmists do. Second best is by touching an object belonging to the person, or handling a photograph of a letter written by the person, or listening to the person's voice on the telephone. Emotional links through a third person also permit psychic contact. The advantage of psychometry, or object-reading, is that one can make psychic contact with a person thousands of miles away.

A good example of this came when a distraught woman visited me to help her find her lost dog. The dog had escaped from a crate at the Chicago airport, from where it was supposed to be shipped to her in Los Angeles. The woman regarded the dog as her closest friend. Psychically I traced the dog's journey from the airport. I saw it leaping into the back of a truck, which took it to a distant area of the city. I advised the woman to check the animal shelter in that area of Chicago. She telephoned me that next day. The dog was there, and was soon reunited with its grateful owner.

In May 1982 I did an experiment in psychometry with Dr Weston Agor, who is now head of the Master of Public Administration Program at the University of Texas at El Paso. At the time of the reading he was at California State, Long Beach, and had an idea for a book on intuitive management. Agor's *Intuitive Management* was published in spring 1984 by Prentice-Hall and contained my reading as a postscript. Dr Agor has updated his annotations, which appear in brackets.[18] I began by asking to hold Agor's ring:

Vaughan: Why don't I start with some things I already know about you and get them out of the way? I think I know that you worked as a management consultant. If you haven't, you will. Now I'm seeing you shifting your position at California State, Long Beach. In the fall this will be. The emphasis of your work will be shifting from there. Occasionally you may teach something there, but your home base is moving I believe. And it will be to a small institute. [WA: *I did move to a new location in the fall of 1982 to Director of the MPA Program at the University of Texas at El Paso.*]

   Oh—I think you will do three papers. [WA: *I did write a few articles in the spring of 1983.*]

   And my feeling is that—you may not want to year this— that your plans for the book will be extended somewhat.

Agor: Delayed, you mean?

Vaughan: Yes, I think you will be doing a first draft of maybe a few chapters, but I think you are going to want to include more information based on some interviews and new studies that are being done. So, it's going to take a bit longer than you think right now.

Agor: Do you still see it coming out though?

Vaughan: Yes—I certainly do! And it looks like it's a hard cover, at least initially. [WA: *The book was accepted for hard cover publication in 1983 for spring 1984 publication.*]

Agor: Do you see Tarcher publishing it?

Vaughan: Tarcher?

Agor: Yes, because I've almost had a feeling that I'm being guided to them.

Vaughan: Well, I'm not sure about that. I wonder if it might be something more like Prentice-Hall—a company that deals more with a list of technical titles. [WA: *It was not Tarcher, as I thought, but Prentice-Hall that published it.*]

   And I think you will be doing a lot of traveling in the fall to Washington. Certainly, to consult about a training program for an agency there. [WA: *I went to the Washington area to do a workshop for the Federal Executive Institute and later several government agencies.*]

Agor: What kind of reception do you see for the book?

Vaughan: Boy, it seems to me being used something like a textbook for several small groups, and then it's going into paper edition. I guess a quality paperback, having a pretty good success. Boy—this sounds far too optimistic to trust, but the figure I just got was 165,000 copies. It seems excessive but... [WA: *The book did come out as a quality paperback. It has been used as a textbook by 50 of the leading management schools, including Harvard, Stanford and Yale, and is being used by a variety of other organizations as well. The sales figure Vaughan gave was far too optimistic but the book has sold well, going through four printings.*]

Agor: I don't know, boy, when you get in that textbook market.

Vaughan: Well—it's not like an undergraduate textbook. That's where the money is. Your book is more like a graduate school book. I think training programs which are not particular affiliated with universities ... companies' organization development. I think you will be working with a large company. I'm thinking of something on the order of IBM—maybe not for the whole company, but one division of it, developing a training program for their employees. It's like a two or three week program they will be going through. But I see the location in Southern California or the Southwest. [WA: *I did work for a number of large companies such as Tenneco, Walt Disney Enterprises, Hawaii Telephone Company, New Jersey Telephone, Arizona City Management Association and large associations such as the International Personnel Management Association. My university department is in the Southwest—El Paso—not California.*]

Agor: This institute that you see me going to in the fall—is it in Southern California?

Vaughan: I believe so. I think it's in Southern California, but I'm not sure where it is. I'm not sure that the institute even exists yet. But, it might well be something—or a new program being created from an established organization—creating a new separate program or institute.

Agor: Could it be something that I set up myself?

Vaughan: Oh yes—it could very well be.

Agor: Because I have been thinking about it.

Vaughan: Although I think there are some other people involved in it ... two or three people. I see you going through a study program of your own, fairly intensive—a situation in which you are trying various kinds of things, kind of impossible things—and having quite good success with this. And being quite amazed at the kinds of things you are able to do. I may be projecting here, but I wonder if I might be connected with that somehow.

Agor: Could be. [WA: *I did work on several new innovative courses in the management program at UTEP, including bringing Vaughan to campus to do a workshop and lecture. I received a national award recently for this work from the Freedoms Foundation in Valley Forge, appeared*

on NBC's Today Show, and have received other national
recognition in Psychology Today, Discover, The New York
Times and the London Times.]

Agor's success in bringing intuition into the corporate world is
indicative of a growing acceptance of intuition in many industries.
Roy Rowan, an editor at *Fortune*, states that over half the Fortune
500 companies now have training programs in the area of
creativity and intuition. It would be a natural development for
these training courses to include the art of psychometry, perhaps
calling it 'right-brain sensing'.

The reason I tape-record my impressions instead of writing them
down directly is that speaking enables me to maintain a flow of
imagery without drawing too much on the left brain as I would
need to do if I were writing; the psychic impressions might be
overpowered by my logical mind.

The biggest advantage of object-reading is that the client does not
have to make an expensive 3,000-mile journey to see me in
person. And an advantage for me is that the client cannot distract
me, argue with me, explain too much, or otherwise break the flow
of impressions. The only disadvantage is that the client must wait
until later before asking additional questions.

Psychometry does not always work. There are many complex
factors involved, such as the person's own psychic ability,
openness and need for the information. It is least likely to work
when you try to prove something to somebody who has no
intrinsic interest or belief in it. It is also possible to be short-
circuited by someone else, especially in group situations.

The very first time I attempted psychometry for a group, I had
people put objects in a basket while I was out of the room. I chose
a woman's wedding ring to give a reading on. I said the woman had
been a nun and now had a daughter. The woman whose ring I held
said that was not true. The woman seated directly behind her
boomed out, 'Everything you said applies to me. I used to be a nun
and now I am married and have a daughter.'

Later, someone told me, 'Oh, that woman is such a psychic
butinsky. Nobody else can get a reading when she's around.'
Indeed, the former nun's powerful personality seemed to extend
also to the psychic level.

It is therefore possible to be short-circuited by someone else
whose psychic field is stronger than the target person. To lessen
the possibility of such short-circuiting—and also to remove the

pressure of speaking before a group—I divide my students into pairs and ask them to give readings for each other. Of thousands of people who have attempted this exercise, over 90 per cent have been successful. Sometimes the information comes in symbolic form; sometimes in highly specific form. It seems to vary with the person read for, as well as with the abilities of the person doing the reading.

How is it possible that we all have a latent talent for sensing information about other people? Where does that information come from? Why does a physical object touched by a person enhance perception of information about him or her? To answer these questions I postulate a field of consciousness (sometimes called a 'psi-field') that directs the physical body and radiates pure consciousness from the body. Any object touched by it or any person emotionally involved in that consciousness field partakes of it; since the consciousness field is holographic, any part of it reproduces the whole, though in imperfect resolution. When we remove our usual barriers and open up to receive information from this consciousness field—or an object touched by the target person—we are able to describe some of the information contained in the field, which can be about the past, the present, or the future. The consciousness field contains the seeds of future events or of *possible futures*. Decoding the information in those seeds— blueprints of life—constitutes a psychic reading.

In working with thousands of students over the past 20 years, I have come to a few conclusions about what facilitates beginning attempts at doing psychic readings. First, there must be a *proper context* of people gathered together for just this purpose. They must be motivated and open to the possibility; the fact that they pay money to be there ensures their motivation. Second, they must be *able to witness* actual demonstrations. Seeing is believing; people tend to believe what they see, and open up to the possibility that they, too, can do it. Third, a *group field of consciousness* is built up, enabling individuals to perform better than if they tried it alone. Generally, results get better as the workshop goes on and this group consciousness develops.

At a workshop at the Human Dimensions Institute in Buffalo, New York, in 1969, a student named Carol Liaros told me she was already practiced at psychometry. So, after my attempts, I asked her to do a few readings in front of the group. She was quite accurate in her impressions. Immediately a chorus came up from the others: 'How did you *do* it?' When one of their own group did psychometry, it was somehow more astonishing. Since that time Carol Liaros has established herself as a teacher in the psychic field and teaches the blind how to use ESP at her own institute.

In Liaros's regular ESP classes, she often does psychic readings for the students, who are then asked to rate her statements as true or false. Too often, though, Carol would find the students viewing themselves in too complimentary a light. When she asked one woman why she had marked a certain statement false, the woman said, 'Oh, that's the way I *used* to be. I'm changing now.' It occurred to Liaros that the only objective way of measuring accuracy of psychic readings would be to predict events for the students. She would attempt to answer three questions about objective events scheduled to happen in the next 12 weeks. The answers would be either yes or no, and would be filed with parapsychologist Douglas Dean, a chemist who did pioneering work testing the precognitive abilities of businessmen.

The questions were basically simple, such as 'Will our union contract be accepted or rejected on Sunday 24 October?' Liaros answered, 'Accepted.' The student who asked this question was surprised by this answer, since he was predicting the contract would be rejected, based on the overall evidence in his union, which had been talking about a strike. On the day before the vote, a complete change of attitude came over the union, and the contract was accepted.

In all, 94 people asked 285 questions. When the final outcomes of the events became known, Dean found that Liaros was 81 per cent correct in her predictions—far more often than the students who made predictions. Paradoxically, the people who were experts about their own lives were unable to predict as accurately as a stranger what the final outcomes would be. Perhaps the students were constrained by their logical minds and found it difficult to use their intuition or ESP because their minds were filled with reason. Liaros, on the other hand, had no facts or logic by which to go, and was forced to use her ESP to get an answer. We know that she wasn't 'reading minds', since her predictions were far more accurate than those of the students. The Liaros-Dean experiment indicates that objectivity, even ignorance, about a situation may set the stage for better use of predictive powers.[19]

Contact with Ourselves

'If someone else can see into your future, so can you' is my favorite way of putting precognition into perspective. If a psychic can tune in to your inner consciousness to glimpse the seeds of your future, you can do the same thing—if you can become *objective* about your own life.

Not everyone wants to see into the future: many people fear it and avoid even thinking about it. They fear death, disaster, heartbreak, failure—anything that might cast a doubt on their rosy fantasies of what will be. We are always hoping that things will turn out the way we wish them to. We have strong feelings about our lives, vested interests to protect, an ego to keep well nourished. But unless we rise above our emotions and ego needs to attain an objectivity about our lives, we will not be able to predict our future with accuracy.

We have a screen that usually prevents us from having direct contact with our future. It is there for a purpose. If we do not know the future we can at least hope for it. It is *hope* that drives us through difficult situations and spurs us to take up challenges we might otherwise not be willing to confront if we knew that failure lay ahead. Yet failure is the best way we have of learning—and the lessons stick with us because it is hard-earned knowledge.

The lessons gained from failure give us strength and resiliency in our pursuit of inner goals. We practice until we get it right. The only *real* failure in life is not to attempt some desired goal out of fear of failure.

When trying to be objective about your future you must realize that it is better for you *not* to know everything; that your inner self reveals to you only that information about the future that can be useful to you now. Your inner self can give you hope, inspiration, creative ideas, plans and aspirations, goals and guiding images. If you begin to believe in those guiding images, you are more likely to attain them. If you begin to develop a sense of your destiny, you will be more likely to fulfill it.

Spontaneous contact with your inner self can occur in a moment of crisis or in a sudden realization, when all is peaceful. It may occur when you are 12 or 26 or 42, or at any time when it is needed. Typically, if my own life is a good example, the same thought will emerge several times before it is finally believed by the conscious mind. You have to be convinced that your destiny is attainable.

My interest in becoming a writer first glimmered through at the age of 10, when I worked in a bookstore. But I shoved the thought into the back of my mind because that seemed like such an unrealistic goal. Just a childish hope, I reasoned—without substance.

It happened again when I was 16, then working in a library, in the order department. I unpacked all the new books and had first choice of those I wanted to read. I read omnivorously, but my interest in science, particularly, was disappointed by the materialistic approach most science writers took. A thought bubbled up in my mind for a moment: 'I would like to write books about the real substance of science and counteract the dogmatic assertions of blind materialism.' But again I repressed the thought. After all, I was only in high school; I didn't really know anything about science, and I had no practice at writing.

When it happened the third time, I took more notice. At the age of 23, when I was studying for a master's degree in library studies at Rutgers, I became quite ill with mononucleosis. As a high fever enveloped me, I decided to walk in the cooling rain. In this feverish state, I experienced a powerful uprush from the inner self that said; 'I do not want to be a librarian. I want to bring books into the world instead of conserving them.'

I took my inner self's advice, left library school without the master's and, after army service, landed a job as a science book editor. I had no experience, but I managed to score highest out of the hundred applicants who took an editorial test.

The final uprush of this theme before it became reality occurred in 1965, when I was 29 and working on chemistry and physics textbooks. I had a bizarre experience in which my brain seemed to be invaded by an alien entity for 24 hours. Since I did not believe in spirits, the experience was acutely painful. Yet suddenly I received a message: '*Each of us has a spirit while living.*' At that moment I became aware of my own spiritual essence, which began to vibrate through my body, expanding and traveling up to my brain. With this extraordinary feeling of extending beyond my skin came the most incredible feeling of well-being I had ever experienced. My spiritual essence, or consciousness field, pushed the alien entity out of my head and continued to expand, leading me into another dimension beyond time and space. For about two hours afterward I was able to perceive thoughts and feelings from others and sense events in the future. I was in contact with my inner self.

My first thought was, maybe I'm going crazy. But if I'm not—and this must have happened to other people—it's more important than any of the science books that I've been editing. As I delved into the field of parapsychology, I found that extraordinary experiences have indeed happened to many people: I resolved to write about my experiences and learn more about these uncanny talents. I enrolled in a writing course, and took my first steps at fulfilling a destiny I had glimpsed, but disbelieved, as a child. I took up the study of parapsychology as a profession and found myself squarely in the middle of the greatest mysteries of science. I had seen it, so I believed it—and could finally disbelieve those clever skeptics who argued away humankind's most extraordinary powers.

I suspect that most of us have intimations of our destiny at a young age but suppress them because our destinies seem to be beyond our skill or attainment. But, somehow, through the years, we manage to accumulate skills and to glean bits and pieces of our destined understanding. With time, our childish dream becomes a mature reality.

Once I had experienced full contact with the inner self and the feeling of vibrant well-being, I was able to recreate it later at will. That feeling of self-transcendence became the model for a type of meditation. Standing upright, since that is how it first happened, with my eyes wide open, I focused my mind on my inner self and let vibrating feelings of energy rise up my body to my head, then above my head. Tingling sensations up and down my spine, which became a constant purr and then pushed into my brain, announced the arrival of the completely altered state. I found that this profound contact with the inner self—and its accompanying feeling of well-being—served well as the initial stage of psychic awareness

I began to experience intimations of the future. When a colleague asked me what disaster would next strike New York City after the subway strike, I predicted the Blizzard of '66 with exact dates for the beginning and end.

Later I began to meditate with eyes closed when I took classes at the College of Psychic Science in London. I kept up the meditation as a way not only to enter a psychic state of mind but also to experience self-healing energies.

The traditional doorway for making contact with the inner self is meditation. When the mind learns to focus attention and quiet distracting chatter from the left brain, an altered state of consciousness arises which can be productive of future sight. Once the mind is trained to focus attention, meditation is no longer necessary when attempting to receive psychic impressions.

How will you know when you find that state of consciousness? When your impressions, feelings, visual imagery, and verbal messages from the inner self correspond to an outer—or future—reality. When you are able to describe something unknown to you and it turns out to be right, you know you are not imagining things. It is, by definition, extra-sensory perception.

In the real world, ESP is not sharply defined and distinct from other types of knowing. Logic, intuition, guessing, hunches all play a part in coming up with the right answer. Since most of my work is now in the real world, I no longer call myself a 'psychic' but an 'intuitive', since the answers may come in many ways. The important thing is to get the right answer.

This is how my intuitive state of consciousness feels: an overall feeling of exhilaration, which is, however, kept in check; a tingling in my forehead, pronounced more on the right side; a feeling of pulsation in my solar plexus combined with a mild excited feeling, as if anticipating something pleasant; above all, an attitude of expectancy that something useful will pop into my head. When this state of consciousness becomes more profound, such a strong feeling of well-being and joy floods over me that it provokes a smile. My senses become heightened and emotions are more deeply felt.

In this state of mind it becomes easier to generate a flow of imagery in the mind's eye. Impressions, both verbal and visual, come quickly in response to questions. Sometimes the anwers are specific; at other times they are symbolic.

Hypnosis is a related state of consciousness that is productive of heightened ESP perception. Over the years I have been hypnotized many times in psychic experiments, but I am coming to believe that the main effect of hypnosis is to give one permission to accomplish the impossible. It operates more on one's belief system than it does on actual production of ESP. Once you believe in your own psychic abilities, hypnosis is no longer necessary; if you can predict your future under hypnosis, you can do it while completely awake.

In reviewing my experiences in making contact with the inner self—through spontaneous uprushes, crises, meditation and hypnosis—I find I prefer the quiet, meditative approach. It is far less painful and works more productively to integrate the ways of the inner self with the conscious self. It is also more productive of future sight.

Restrictions

In talking with about a hundred psychics and others who have experienced precognition, I have concluded that the inner self puts restrictions on what may be foreseen. An anecdote told me by a Dutch writer illustrates this restriction.

In the 1950s, when the writer was researching a book on the Dutch psychic Gerard Croiset—probably the world's most gifted precognitive psychic—he was approached by an Italian casino owner who wanted to try psychic prediction as an experiment at the horse races. So the writer, Croiset and the casino owner journeyed to a race track near Paris for the experiment. Croiset extracted a promise from the casino owner that he would not bet on any of Croiset's predictions. That condition met, Croiset took a racing program and checked off his choices for the winners in seven races. Against astronomical odds, all seven horses came in.

The casino owner was stunned. He proposed that they stay one more day and repeat the experiment. Croiset said, 'Now promise you won't bet.'

'I won't bet,' promised the casino owner.

The next morning, as before, Croiset checked off his choices for seven races. The first horse lost. The second horse lost. When the third horse came in a loser, Croiset turned to the casino owner and said, 'You bet, didn't you?'

'Yes, I bet. I'm sorry. I just couldn't resist,' confessed the casino owner.

The inner self puts *moral restrictions* on psychic perception. Money, like experience, must be earned. Others have told me of winning at the track or other gambling situations, but usually the winnings amounted to exactly what they needed—and not a dollar more. I have never heard of multi-millionaire psychics who made it by gambling. When greed becomes the motivation for use of psychic talents, the talents disappear.

Contact with the Future

In formal experiments in time, the late Gerard Croiset was without peer. Professor W.H.C. Tenhaef in Holland, Professor Hans Bender in Germany, and Dr Jule Eisenbud in the United States were his chief investigators in analyzing chair tests. A chair test is a prediction experiment in which the subject attempts to describe in detail a person whose seat number will be chosen at random at a public hall. A number of Croiset's chair tests have been quantitatively analyzed to give high odds against chance. On a qualitative level they are impressive because of the amount of accurate detail Croiset was able to foresee about the target persons.

Important for us, though, is how Croiset made contact with those unknown persons. I believe it was through Croiset's own future experience of making contact with them at the final stage of the chair test, when the people whose numbers were drawn came up on the stage to listen to a tape recording of Croiset's predictions. Croiset had to be there, too.

This first occurred to me when I witnessed a chair test in Zurich, Switzerland, on 6 May 1968. I had been present a few days before when Croiset recorded his predictions in Freiburg, Germany. Croiset complained that there was going to be confusion. He described a woman and included such details as her stealing a plant from someone's garden and that someone smashing a window in her home. Then Croiset began to talk about a man who did judo and was over six feet tall. Yet only *one* number was to be chosen at this experiment.

In Zurich the target person was chosen by randomly drawing counters from a basket; it turned out to be the woman Croiset had described. She visibly blushed when the recording revealed her secret about the plant theft and swift retribution. But then a man jumped up on the stage and began to translate Croiset's shaky German into more proper German. At this point the recording switched to the description of the six-footer who did judo. It was the man who had jumped on stage.

It became evident that Croiset could have given the same information if he were just asked to describe someone whom he would meet on the evening of 6 May 1968. All that shuffling of random numbers to come up with the target person was beside the point. Croiset was making contact with his own future—getting feedback to his psychic responses.

In January 1969, Croiset was filmed in Holland while he made predictions about two people who were to be chosen by a complex random system at a hall in Denver, Colorado, a few weeks later. He described a woman who had an emotional experience dealing with page 64 of a book she was reading. His description of a man included the unusual detail of his having a coat with green spots caused by a chemical from his work in a scientific laboratory.

A few weeks later in Denver, Jule Eisenbud advertised for potential target people by offering a free lecture and experiment in ESP. Those who made it through a snowstorm that night were all given questionnaires to fill out in response to Croiset's statements. Then the random selection was made. The target woman had been upset by page 64 of a book that discussed putting cats to sleep. The target man's lab coat did indeed have spots on it. Ordinarily the spots were not visible, but in the special light he used in his lab, the spots glowed green.

Eisenbud had the Denver proceedings filmed and added the Dutch footage for a film that he has available for rental. Croiset saw the film three months after it was made and received feedback on his predictions. He made contact with his future.[20]

Let us set up some optimal situations in which we can practice prediction. There is only one caveat: do not be afraid of making mistakes. the worst you can be is wrong.

Exercises

Psychometry or Object Reading

1. Find someone to act as a target person. It should be a stranger or someone you don't know well. You might meet at a dinner party, waiting at an airport, or at a doctor's office. Tell your target person that you are practicing developing your ESP. The target person should respond to your statement with a simple yes or no about their accuracy. Ask the target person for some object to hold—a watch, a ring, a comb, a wallet—or simply touch the person if that situation is comfortable. Make sure you will not be disturbed.

2. Begin your reading by telling the person what you have already learned about him or her. This gets the logical information out of the way. Now open your mind to anything at all—pictures, words, symbols—and tell the person what you see and hear. After these initial impressions, ask yourself: what sort of work does the person do, what are his or her family members like, where does the person live, what is his or her emotional life like now? As you talk, pay attention to the imagery forming in your mind's eye. If you are beginning to 'get hot', the person will agree to some of your statements. If you are wrong, shift the line of self-questioning. If you are correct in some of your statements, you are getting tuned in to the person and can proceed to the future.

3. Now ask the target person if he or she has any questions about events in his or her future. It should be something fairly important to the person, objective in nature, and not far away

in time. Now you may want to attempt additional predictions
if you feel you are in contact with the target person. Ask the
person to telephone you when the outcome of the future event
is known.

The Mysterious Stranger

1. The next time you plan to meet with a stranger (a blind date
    would be perfect), try to picture in your mind's eye what the
    stranger will look like. Sketch the person. What color eyes and
    hair does he or she have? Any predominant facial features?
    How tall? How will he or she be dressed? What is his or her
    personality like? Ask yourself questions about the stranger—
    the same questions you will ask when you meet in person.

2. When you finally meet the stranger, compare your impres-
    sions of his or her appearance with the way he or she looks.
    Now engage the person in conversation and ask the very
    questions you asked yourself earlier. Find out if any of your
    impressions are accurate. Mention that you are reading a book
    on prediction. If the stranger seems interested, you might want
    to reveal your precognitive impressions and sketch. If
    the person is not interested, do not mention your little
    experiment. The advantage of this exercise over many others is
    that the mysterious stranger never need know that he or she
    was the object of a psychic experiment. And if you are wrong,
    the person will never know!

5.

Guiding Images

From our dreams, meditations, and spontaneous uprushes we receive glimpses of our future—guiding images from our inner self. These guiding images come to sustain us when we reach a crossroads of life and must make a major decision that will direct the course of our future. By making an effort to understand our guiding images—and acting on them—we can fulfill our destiny.

Guiding Dreams

My first guiding dream came to me when I was becoming interested in psychic and spiritual development. I was wondering if it might be possible to pursue a career in parapsychology. Where might it lead? The answer came in a dream of 26 January 1966:

A Trip in a Rocket Ship

I was graduating from high school and, for my excellence, was awarded a trip in a rocket ship. I was concerned about the propulsion system—I didn't want to go in it until I found out what made it go.

To get to the rocket ship I had to cross a bridge. There were three lanes, one wide, one medium, and one narrow. I took the narrow one on the left; it was very bumpy. Two others and I went across in a toboggan. We had to hold on very tightly, and the ride was very bumpy. At the end of the slide we crashed into a bookcase, from which fell out some books. One fell into my lap—it explained the propulsion system. I felt elated.

Attempting to interpret the dream, I wrote down possible meanings of the symbols: 'The high school represents basic learning about life. The rocket ship is higher knowledge. The propulsion system may equal the spiritual force of higher knowledge. The bridge represents the paths leading to knowledge.

A decision must be made to choose one. The left, narrow lane is the most difficult—dangerous but the fastest. I shall have to undergo many difficulties, perhaps fearing for my own sanity. The book on propulsion stands for wisdom and understanding of spiritual forces. I shall finally, even dramatically, find it.'

The dream guided me into explorations of consciousness and seemed to be fulfilled many years later. Looking back on the dream, I can see more easily how it symbolically forecast my adventures in parapsychology. My concern about not wanting to go on the rocket ship before learning about the propulsion system accurately described my attitude of wanting to know the theoretical basis for precognition. There was also a literal element, since I learned much in making a series of predictions about the rocket ships sent to the moon in the Apollo missions. I closely identified with space exploration, and even gave my high-school graduating ambition in life as 'Being the first man on the moon.'

The fast, bumpy ride with two others that ended with a book accurately forecast my personal psychic experiences and laboratory work, which I wrote up in collaboration with two others in the book *Dream Telepathy*. It proposed theoretical ideas on psychic functioning, which I took further in my later books, *Patterns of Prophecy* and *Incredible Coincidence*, to develop a general theory of psychic phenomena and the underlying principles of precognition. When I visited the Manned Spacecraft Center in Houston five years after the dream, Apollo 14 astronaut Edgar Mitchell let me play out my dream in a trip in a training capsule for the Apollo missions.

For me, the importance of the dream lay not so much in any literal correspondences with the future but in the inspiring images that guided me and helped me make the major decision to enter parapsychology. The dream convinced me that my life's fulfillment could be reached by investigation of the theoretical principles that power higher knowledge. It also warned me that a bumpy ride was ahead. I soon left my job as a science editor and embarked on a voyage through time in search of that dream.

How might you recognize a guiding dream when it comes? First, consider the context of your life. If you are feeling dissatisfied or sensing that life no longer holds the excitement and challenge it once did, it may mean that you are about to make a major change. It may come when you have a major decision to make and when you call up your dream tiger for guidance.

Some characteristics of guiding dreams include positive emotion, especially at the dream's conclusion, symbolic imagery that has both a universal and personal meaning, and a goal that promises fulfillment.

A parapsychological colleague and friend, Jeffrey Mishlove, told me how a guiding dream put him on his present path. In 1980 Mishlove was awarded a Ph.D. in parapsychology by the University of California at Berkeley. It was a long and arduous study program. Mishlove even had to create his own interdisciplinary parapsychology faculty, transferring from the Department of Criminology. This major change in Mishlove's life direction began when he called up his dream tiger:

In 1972, while I was a student in criminology at the University of California, I was also a conscientious objector—and in desperate need (I then believed) of finding alternative service work to fulfill my draft requirement. This was hard to find and was causing me a great deal of worry. My life, as a whole, seemed very unsettled at the time.

In order to resolve this dilemma, I decided to program a dream to provide me with an answer.

I dreamed that I went to visit some friends who lived in married student housing at Berkeley. They were not home, but knowing where they kept the key, I found it and let myself in. On the floor of the living room was a magazine called *Eye*, which I picked up and looked through. It was in that magazine, I dreamed, that I would find the answer to my problems.

So the very next morning I got up and jogged over to my friends' apartment at married student housing. They were not home, but finding the key I let myself in. There, in the middle of the living room floor, was a magazine. *Focus*, the publication of KQED, a listener-sponsored radio and television station in San Francisco. It provided a focus for me, as I had the sudden realization while reading it that I would like to find alternative service work in listener-sponsored, educational media.

I found a job at KPFA-FM in Berkeley, the oldest listener-sponsored radio station in the United States. Within three weeks, I was given my own bi-weekly radio program, *The Mind's Ear*, which opened many doors for me. My life felt together, centered. I had found my place in the universe.

Mishlove's next radio program was called *Roots of Consciousness*, for which he interviewed parapsychologists and consciousness researchers. Next he wrote a book of the same title, and that was the first stage toward getting his doctorate in parapsychology. He is now doing a television series for PBS called *Thinking Allowed*.

Mishlove's guiding dream provided a literal precognition of his finding the *Focus* magazine (instead of *Eye*, which focuses). The paranormal impact of this find led him to consider deeply what answer the magazine migh suggest. If he had not had the dream predicting finding the magazine, he might have just leafed through it and not thought about it.

The guiding dream may not give the answer directly but may point to where it can be found. Note how the life event, like a dream, symbolically stated that Mishlove would find *focus* in his life.

Editor-publisher Eleanor Friede, who has her own imprint with Delacorte Press, told in an interview in *Psychic* magazine how a dream provided the answer to her question about a major career change in 1971. As a newly appointed editor at Macmillan, with publicity experience, she was asked by Macmillan to reorganize and head the publicity department for a while. Not wanting to return to publicity work, she agonized over the decision for two weeks. The day before her answer was due she had a vivid dream in which she saw herself happy as a lark, with an enthusiastic staff and a bank of offices in a special corner section. She awoke happy and reported in to accept the position.

Shortly afterwards, the department was moved to a different floor. 'It was the exact corner in my dream, the same layout and number of people, with bright lights and all,' she recalls. 'I think now I really saw my successor, and that I was a necessary force to put her there. It was a right move, which I didn't know until I saw it in the dream.'[21]

Typical of guiding dreams, Eleanor Friede's dream not only gave her the guidance she sought but also previsioned some actual details of the future once she acted on her dream's advice. When I visited her at her dreamed-of corner office at Macmillan in 1972, she told me of many other intuitive, psychic experiences that had given her the conviction that she should follow her dreams.

Friede's most celebrated accomplishment in the book trade was signing a little book that many other publishers had rejected. At Macmillan the other editors teased her about 'Friede's Folly'. *Publishers Weekly* dismissed it as 'ickypoo'. But Friede was determined to follow her intuition and guided the book into stratospheric sales of more than 24 million copies around the world. Richard Bach's *Jonathan Livingston Seagull* had originally come to the writer in a series of dreamlike experiences, and in reality became the biggest seller since *Gone with the Wind*. Both

Friede and Bach were following their dreams.

Tapping the Blueprints of Life

Even as dreams tap our deep inner self for guiding images, psychics can tap the guiding images of our lives, revealing to us future possibilities we may be unaware of or are unsure of. The important thing for us is to evaluate those images to determine if they are truly guiding images or if they come from *strongly held fantasies*.

When I undertook a series of experiments with British mediums in 1967–8, my first wife, Iris, often accompanied me and took notes of their predictions. Since she was there, the psychics often predicted events for her as well as for me. They were often uncanny in telling her she would do exactly what she held strong fantasies about: becoming an opera singer. Not a single prediction made for Iris ever came true.

As she realizes now, she had neither the vocal equipment nor the dedicated determination needed to become an opera personality. The psychics were not tapping her deep inner self but were merely feeding back to her strongly held fantasies of her conscious mind. Iris had determined to become an opera singer as a child of five, and the goal was reinforced when a friend of hers signed a contract with the Metropolitan Opera.

The British mediums' predictions for me, on the other hand, often did come true. Usually their predictions surprised me because I had no conscious plans or wishes in that regard, but when I heard the predictions—the ones that were later fulfilled—they felt right. They seemed to be guiding images toward which I could work. The predictions included these major points of my life: I would move to California and write for a magazine on psychic phenomena; I would become a lecturer and teacher; I would write books on psychic phenomena, including one co-authored by two others; I would develop my own psychic and healing abilities; I would do radio broadcasting (over 300 radio shows so far); I would write for movies or television (I'm working on it).

For me those predictions became guiding images, and when opportunities arose for going in those directions, I seized them. They were congruent with the images of my life's blueprints, and became self-fulfilling prophecies.

Artificial Dreaming

I have an exercise called *artificial dreaming* for those who have trouble remembering their dreams. It has proved a popular class exercise. An artificial dream is a psychic reading for someone, cast in the form of a dream or a fairy tale. It tells a story, it has symbolic meanings, it can be illogical and cut to new scenes without explanation. Since it is meant to be prophetic, the artificial dream is cast in the present and future, and emphasizes the positive aspects of life. The artificial dreamer casts the person dreamed about as the hero or heroine of the story and engages in the creative act of storytelling—which also engages ESP.

When artificial dreaming is done for someone else, there is often a mixture of the storyteller's projection and ESP about the protagonist—sometimes revealing guiding images. It is also a great deal of fun for the person making up the story. Since getting started is the hardest part, I recommend that the storyteller begin with a children's tale, since archetypal qualities suit such tales to universal symbolism. Afterwards, the person dreamed about can sort out the symbolism and discover what guiding images may be present in the artificial dream.

I also suggest that people make up artificial dreams for themselves. By getting caught up in the creative act of storytelling and depending on symbols, they are able to get around the logical mind to tap guiding images from the inner self. Once the story gets underway images begin to appear in the mind's eye and the story tells itself, often wandering far from its beginning.

Here is an artificial dream I made up for myself at a recent workshop just before Easter:

The Secret of Time

I become Jack in the Beanstalk. I plant a seed in the ground and one night the full moon shines on it and a great beanstalk grows through the clouds. I climb up the beanstalk and poke my head through the little cloud. To my surprise I find a dozen golden eggs. I find a basket and put the golden eggs in the basket. I look around now and expect to see a castle and a giant. I don't see a castle. But far in the distance is a beautiful tower. As I get closer I find it is the tower of time.

As I approach the tower of time, I see a little door at the base. There is a turnstile, and I must deposit one of my golden eggs for admission. I do this and climb one storey. There is another turnstile, and so I deposit another golden egg. In this way I climb 11 storeys and deposit 11 eggs. When I reach the top of the tower of time, I find a special niche that is just right for the last golden egg.

When I put the final golden egg in place in the niche, there is a
fanfare of trumpets and drums. The clock face of time becomes alive
and says, 'You may now ask any question.'

'What is the secret of time?' I ask.

The clock face smiles and says, 'Time will tell.' I start laughing.

There was an interesting correspondence to an event the very next
day when my family went to visit the Galleria in Glendale so that
our small children could see the Easter bunny. On top of the Easter
bunny's pavillion were about a dozen giant eggs. At the other end
of the gallery (which I had never before visited) was a beautiful
clock tower, which had an uncanny resemblance to the tower of
time in my artificial dream.

Symbolically, the 12 golden eggs represent the 12 chapters of the
original edition of this book. Perhaps when we reach the eleventh
story, or chapter (new Chapter 12), we shall find the secret of time.

Becoming One Another

Sometimes we see ourselves most clearly through the eyes of
another. If you have ever had the impulse to tell someone, 'If I were
you, I would ...' then you will recognize the advantage of
temporarily becoming someone else. This popular exercise in
future consciousness could not be simpler. Two people who do
not know much about each other are paired off and each assumes
the identity of the other. Taking turns, about 10 minutes apiece,
each person introduces himself or herself in this new identity and
talks about the things that are important to him or her. Then the
other person questions him or her about attitudes and goals in life.

Let's say our two people are Sue and Mack. Mack says, 'My name
is Sue. I'm married, I work in a stationery store, but I would rather
be an artist. Work at the store bores me but when I think of
creating my own designs, I get excited....'

The real Sue, now the pseudo-Mack, might say, 'Sue, that's very
interesting. Do you think you really have any talent or is this just
a pipe dream because you're so bored?'

Mack, the pseudo-Sue, might answer, 'I think I really do have
talent, but I haven't done much with it. Maybe it's because I devote
so much time to my family that I just haven't found the time to do
things *I* want to do....'

And so on. The dialogue can reveal not only attitudes, situations,
and talents but can also sometimes help someone discover true

guiding images. By attempting to look at yourself through someone else's eyes—someone who must be using ESP if he says correct things about you—a new perspective gives much food for thought, and, occasionally, flashes of enlightenment. The becoming-one-another exercise can also be fun, since it engages creative ability, acting ability, and, ideally, psychic ability.

As with the artificial dreaming exercise, it is up to you to discern what might be projection from the other person and what might truthfully apply to you. Often you will find that the other person will be most accurate when the two of you are alike in some respect. People who try this tell me that they find it unusually stimulating and they really learn some new things about themselves.

The best results from such exercises come when people are able to merge consciousness with each other. If you are successful at getting accurate imagery about the other person, it means that you have been able to suppress your own sense of ego and assume the identity of the other person. You become one with them. It is in this state of communal consciousness that you will best be able to tap the other person's inner self for the guiding images he needs.

Sifting the False from the True

False images of our future arise from our ego needs and masquerade as images from the inner self. Daydreams of power, wealth, fame, success, sexual conquests and so on—you recognize them—have a way of insinuating themselves into our predictions for ourselves. They are also the stock-in-trade of the fortune-teller who knows that a satisfied client is one who is told what he or she wants to hear.

A mature person knows from personal experience that daydream images don't work—their allure is false. But younger people still have these lessons to learn. They are very much in the process of discovering who they are and who they will be. They are learning to sift the false images of self—which are dictated by parents, educators, and society's daydreams—from the true guiding images of their inner self that can bring them fulfillment.

To hasten this process of self-understanding, I offer some guidelines for sifting false from true predictions about oneself. I have fooled myself often enough to be sensitive to these questions:

1.   Does your prediction solve all your problems at one stroke?

Do you foresee that you will win the Irish sweepstakes, inherit a fortune, write the nation's number one best-seller, be a rock star, be a movie star, win the Nobel Prize, marry a millionaire, find a gold mine, or any of a thousand other things you may have heard about that have made other people rich, famous or successful at one stroke? If so, your prediction is probably wrong. You are conjuring up a false image from society's daydreams.

2. Does your prediction include a lot of *ifs*? If so, it is probably drawn from your ego-centered logical mind, which is forever scheming about future possibilities by computing hoped-for odds and calculating optimum chances. There is no *if* about true guiding images; they are not conditional. They just *are*.

3. Is your prediction borrowed from someone else's life? Did a friend accomplish something, and now you want to as well? Does your prediction fulfill your parents' hopes for you? Although we sometimes are inspired to follow the example of others, we must discover whether or not their guiding image is truly ours. More often than not, what works for them will not work for us, because we have our own personal destiny and our own personal guiding images.

4. Would the fulfillment of your prediction give you great satisfaction because you have worked for it? If so, it is probably a true guiding image, provided that you are the sole judge of your satisfaction and do not depend on others to give you recognition.

5. Does your prediction of some hoped-for goal depend on many others for fulfillment? The more people you must depend on to fulfill your prediction, the less likely it is a true guiding image. True guiding images tend to project only what *you* must do; how others may help rarely figures in. However, do not rule out that hoped-for goal. Once you begin fulfilling your part of the prediction, you may find that others begin to help you.

6. Do you have the talents and inner resources to fulfill your prediction? If you answer yes because you have already tested those talents and have already shown those inner resources, your prediction is probably drawn from a true guiding image. If you cannot think of a single time during which those talents or resources manifested themselves, you may have borrowed the image from someone else. If you are not sure, put them to the test as soon as possible to find out. Bear in mind that

talents develop only through practice, that an inner resource is like a muscle that must be exercised before it grows strong.

7. Does your prediction include a plan for fulfillment? If the plan is a general strategy that requires work on your part, it is probably a true guiding image. If the prediction includes precise details of who is to do what and when, it probably springs from the ego-centered logical mind. Usually guiding images from the inner self concentrate on the final picture— the goal— but do not tell you exactly how to get there. That you must discover at the necessary time.

8. Does your prediction relate to an outcome that you have not thought about before but that stimulates a good feeling? If so, you are probably tapping a true guiding image. Your feelings are the true measure of your inner self's guiding images.

9. Does your prediction massage your ego at the expense of accomplishment? If you see yourself getting acclaim but have no idea what work you need to accomplish in return for that acclaim, you are probably tapping a false image.

10. Do you predict for yourself an ideal love-mate and think about only what they will do for you and how they will love you? If so, it is probably a daydream. If you foresee how you will be able to help and love them, you may be tapping a true guiding image. If you foresee both of you helping and loving each other, you may be already sharing consciousness with that person—even though you have not yet met.

11. Does your prediction give you a profound feeling of satisfaction and accomplishment when you contemplate its fulfillment? If so, it is probably a true guiding image of your personal destiny. When your inner self seems to glow with quiet anticipation and good feelings, it is a signal that your prediction will be self-fulfilling.

12. Can anyone else tell better than you whether your self-predictions are drawn from false or true images? If you think so, think again. You are the highest authority on your life's predictions and your life's meaning. Only you can best sift your false images from the true.

Exercises

Analyze your Guiding Dreams

1. If you keep a dream diary or have had success at programming dreams by calling up your dream tiger, select a dream that

seems to promise some hoped-for goal in life. The dream may even be a repeating dream from childhood or perhaps just a half-remembered dream that made an impression on you. The dream should have a positive ending and evoke elation or some similar emotion.

2. Translate the symbols of your dream into a basic story of your future. Does the dream seem to indicate a major change in attitudes or professional goals?

3. Might the dream symbols contain some literal elements of your future? Try to identify any important correspondences with your reality that may have already happened.

4. Are the dream symbols drawn from past experience? Were those good experiences or promising ones?

5. In your mind's eye witness the conclusion of the dream and pay attention to the emotion that is evoked. If there is a strong positive emotion, let the dream image inspire and guide you. Return to that guiding image in your mind whenever you doubt you will get where you want to go.

Artificial Dreaming for Others

1. Find a stranger or casual acquaintance for a target person at a dinner party or some social event. Make sure you will not be interrupted. Tell that person you are going to make up a dream about his present and future, which he will have to interpret.

2. Let your imagination have free rein as you make up a story or dream about the other person. You may wish to start with some children's tale with the target person as protagonist. You are free to be as illogical as you like in your creative storytelling. Be entertaining and concentrate on positive aspects of the future as you improvise your artificial dream.

3. Now ask the target person for his interpretation. Does it make any sense to him? Does it correspond at all to the person's life situation? Are the symbols well chosen? What outcome does the artificial dream seem to predict for that person?

4. Now reverse the roles and ask the other person to make up an artificial dream for you. Give him feedback about any correct details and interpret the symbols for him. Are there symbols or themes that particularly appeal to you as possibilities in your life? Record them and later consider them in the light of the questions in the section earlier in this chapter, 'Sifting the False from the True'.

For Yourself

1. Find an audience to whom you will tell an artificial dream for yourself. It could be one person or a group you feel comfortable with, so you can say what you feel. Using yourself as protagonist, make up a story about your future. Regard it as an exercise in creativity—therefore you cannot be 'wrong'. Get caught up in the creative rush of your words and don't worry about what will come up next. Images will form in your mind's eye and show the rest of the dream to you. *Don't attempt to analyze it while you are telling the dream*. This should be an enjoyable experience for you and entertaining for your audience. Be positive.

2. With the help of your audience, try to analyze the dream. Look for themes or incidents that appeal to you. Are there any possible predictions for you? Were there surprises for you in the dream? If there seem to be guiding images, review them with the questions in the section 'Sifting the False from the True'.

Becoming One Another

1. Find a target person whom you do not know well. Tell that person you will play a game in which you assume each other's identity. To start, announce yourself in your new identity and say what you already know about the target person. Then say anything that pops into your head; it could be about the person's attitudes, present life situation, what he or she hopes to do in the future. Make sure that the target person knows that he can ask questions, and before long you will have a dialogue with the identities reversed.

2. Now reverse the roles and let the other person become you. Ask questions about yourself. Does the other person seem to describe you accurately? Does he give you suggestions about your future? Do you have a positive emotional reaction to some of the other person's predictions? If so, they might be guiding images.

3. Did you find that you and the target person are alike in some ways? Explore your common life situations and attitudes. Did you gain any insights about yourself and your possible future?

Acting on It

If you discovered any true guiding images in your explorations, think about how you might act on them.

6.

The Art of Prophecy

The prediction of public events—what I term *prophecy*—requires both psychic and logical insights. It is important to realize that one can prophesy only about possible futures.

Many prophecies are triggered by the dramatic impact of extraordinary news events, events which disrupt our emotions and stir our psyches to sense the next stages in the unfolding drama.

Interpreting Dreams

When the awful news of Robert Kennedy's assassination reached me in Germany in June 1968, my personal grief was compounded because my warning premonition had not been able to prevent that tragedy. As I studied British newspaper accounts of Robert Kennedy's funeral, and a photo of his son, Joseph, then 15, filing past the coffin, I seemed to make psychic contact with Joseph.

The contact extended to Edward Kennedy when I read a journalist's speculations on 'The Fate of the Dynasty'[22]:

> The Kennedys have become, it seems to me, a dangerous American obsession, almost an invitation, if not a provocation, to lunatic acts of violence. They have become like one of those old British families with a legendary curse on the heir. It may just be superstition, but the superstition itself induces an unhealthy atmosphere which helps to perpetuate the legend. The drama of the Kennedys and the Presidency is a play that has gone on long enough, and if Edward Kennedy tries to make a third act of it, then it really is tempting the devil.

Thousands of miles away from home, I wondered how the American people felt about the possibility of Ted Kennedy seeking the presidency. And would Joseph Kennedy become the heir to the

Kennedy dynasty? Would it be cursed? On 13 June, I awoke with a dream:

JFK Returns to Life

President John Kennedy had returned to life, and was again seeking the presidency. I was not a supporter, though I wasn't really against him. We waited for buses to take us to the campaign dinner. There were three places for the buses, one for each campaign. The first waiting place was very long; the other two were short. The group waiting at the last stop were so small that John decided to drive up there in his car. Three others and I then went to dinner with John Kennedy.

There was also my college classics professor, with whom I spoke of Latin. At the dinner party JFK was very charming. He gave us each something he had created. From some protoplasmic material his hand fashioned a nice piece of art. As he was taking me and another young man back to the car, I had to admit I thought he was the best. The young man moved up and sat in the car to my right as if there were a seat facing sideways toward us, somewhat forward. We drove past a storefront, seemingly linked with another past campaign, but it was shut. I remember a sign, something like, 'Would John F. Kennedy Make Pres ... ident Again?'

I wrote down my interpretation of the dream symbols and my associations: 'Yesterday I was wondering if the Kennedy family would one day become a ruling dynasty over America. I was (and am) somewhat hesitant about the idea. The dream seems to be precognitive and is linked with an earlier dream of 8 June, in which John Kennedy's "kid brother" learns the dance of life in politics. Perhaps then Ted Kennedy will again seek the presidency. The three bus stops: the first long one represents JFK's presidency, the second short one represents Robert's campaign attempt, the third one, Ted's campaign in the future. The talk with my classics professor about Latin might be connected with his talks about the emperors of ancient Rome and the dynasties of ancient Egypt. Kennedy creating something artful and nice-looking seems a good sign indeed. The gap in the word *Pres ... ident* means perhaps a gap between the Kennedy presidencies. The closed storefront relating to a previous campaign seems to represent Robert Kennedy's now closed campaign. The young man in the car with us may be yet another Kennedy who will be brought along into the fore (Bobby's son Joseph?) For it was with him that I noticed the closed storefront.'

My first attempt at prophesying from the dream turned out to be wrong—a 1971 prediction that Ted Kennedy would be elected president in 1976. In 1979, however, when polls showed Ted Kennedy the popular favorite as the next Democratic candidate for president, I took another look at the dream and realized my mistake. The dream did not say he would *win* the presidency, only that his campaign would be short. Ted's bus stop had the fewest supporters of all. Although he had grown wise in the dance of politics and was creating something good for us, the dream seemed to predict that he would withdraw from the presidential race.

On 23 October 1979 I registered with the Central Premonitions Registry the prediction 'Senator Ted Kennedy will drop out of the presidential race in 1980.' I estimated the time as 'possibly around February 1980'. The prediction was published in *The Star* on 13 November 1979, and contradicted the majority of presidential predictions: 'According to the psychics, Ted Kennedy will be a sweep.'

In February the first cries came for Kennedy's withdrawal from the presidential race, but he held on until the night before the first ballot at the Democratic convention. When Kennedy's forces lost a rules-change ballot, he officially withdrew his name from nomination.

My 1968 dream also seemed to predict that Ted Kennedy will assist in the future presidential campaign of Joseph Kennedy. If Joseph repeats the pattern of John Kennedy, it could come as early as 1996 when Joseph will be 43 years old—the age at which John won the presidency. The final outcome was posed as a question in my dream: 'Will a Kennedy make president again?'

If the dream is truly prophetic of the next stage of this drama, we can breathe a sigh of relief that there is, at least at this point, no sign of that legendary curse on the heir.

Estimating the date for the fulfillment of a prophetic dream is extremely difficult. I recently discovered, however, a relationship that might prove to be a valuable tool in working with precognitive dreams. The formula is simple: if there is an element from the past in the dream, the future event will be that many years in the future. For example, in my dream 'JFK Returns to Life' there is a reference to my college classics professor and the Latin language. I took Latin in 1956 and 1957, which is 11 to 12 years before the 1968 dream; therefore (I should have realized) it predicted that Ted Kennedy would seek the presidency 11 to 12 years *after* the dream—in 1979 or 1980.

This insight into past and future dream time was triggered by the work of precognition researcher Fred Blau of Sebastapol, California. In tracing time elements from the past and future in his dreams, Blau found a symmetry between the past and future. It occurred to me that if such a symmetry exists *in the same dream*, it might prove a key to the elusive future time. In checking out already fulfilled prophetic dreams that contain datable elements from the past, I have found this relationship to hold up.

As a novice writer, I recorded this promising dream on 25 May 1970:

> I was showing someone poems of mine that I had only just discovered were printed in a 1959 magazine. And then I saw a new issue of *Reader's Digest* that had two poems printed, one by me and one by someone else I knew.

In August 1979 *Reader's Digest* published an article on coincidence ('Coincidence: Is It Black Magic or Blind Chance?' by Edward Ziegler), which included material from my book *Incredible Coincidence* and material from books by Arthur Koestler, whom I knew.

A further fulfillment of the dream happened in 1982, when *Reader's Digest* published a book, *Mysteries of the Unexplained*. I did not see the book until 1985 and was astonished to find that it quoted many of my cases from *Incredible Coincidence*, including a poem-like case titled 'Lucky Seven'. I asked my agent to query *Reader's Digest* about permission fees and received a thousand dollars.

That situation exactly paralleled my original association to the dream; I had written a science-fiction story in high school and was astonished to find it published many years later without my permission. Subtracting 1959 from 1979 gives 11 years; adding 11 to 1970 gives 1981—an approximate average of the years 1979 and 1982 when *Reader's Digest* published the excerpts.

When attempting to interpret a dream about the future, you should keep in mind several basic clues:

1. If the dream itself refers to the future or the subject of precognition, it is probably prophetic.
2. Your associations to the dream elements—what they remind you of—should be considered a part of the dream.

3. Life events just before and after the dream may also be part of the prophetic experience and should be considered when making a prediction. Your associations to these life events may also be important.

4. If your dream is prophetic of some event near in time, it may also predict later fulfillments of that pattern in your life.

Here is an example of a prophetic dream from my own life. Its fulfillment was witnessed by millions of people but its significance was important mainly to me.

The experience began on 13 March 1972, while I was writing *Patterns of Prophecy*. While puzzling over the semantic problem of *precognition* versus *prophecy*, I received a telephone call from parapsychologist Chuck Honorton, at Maimonides Dream Laboratory, about an article on precognition in *Playboy*.

Honorton told me of a dream in which he and I were appearing on the Johnny Carson show. I had had a similar dream recently. But my association to Honorton's dream was a humorous dialogue he had with my first wife, Iris, when she was a subject in an experiment. She had dreamed about Johnny Carson and David Frost, both hosts of TV talk shows. Iris kept referring to Johnny Frost. Finally, Chuck burst out laughing and said, 'Jack Frost!'

That dialogue was my primary association to Honorton's dream, so I felt that the dream might refer to the *David Frost Show* instead of Johnny Carson's *Tonight Show*, which was produced on the West Coast. The *David Frost Show* was produced in New York City, where I lived then. So I registered this prediction with Robert Nelson, director of the Central Premonitions Registry: 'Here's a prediction you will be able to check personally on TV. Charles Honorton and I and someone else (you?) will appear on a nationwide talk show on TV. I think it will be the *David Frost Show*.... Both Chuck and I have had dreams about appearing on the Johnny Carson show, but I think this is an association with the *David Frost Show*.'

A few days later I was astonished to receive a telephone call from a producer of the *David Frost Show*. The show wanted to interview some parapsychologists and psychic subjects, such as myself, who worked in laboratories. Dr Stanley Krippner, Honorton's colleague at Maimonides Dream Laboratory, had agreed to appear on the show and had recommended they contact me. Instead of Honorton, his colleague Krippner appeared on the show with me. It was aired on 28 April, just a few weeks after my prediction. Since then Honorton has appeared on a number of national TV shows, as have I and Robert Nelson.

Sometimes prophetic dreams contain a future time designation that is somewhat scrambled. For instance, two years before my son Thomas was born I had a dream in which my wife and I were worried about our boy growing too fast; he was only two years old and was already six feet tall. I construed that to mean that in two years we would have a baby boy who would grow to be quite tall. He seems to be fulfilling that prediction.

When analyzing your dreams for possible clues about time, pay attention to numbers. Play with them and see if they might be translated into prophetic time units.

In general, to make use of dreams as prophecy it is absolutely necessary to record them and review them periodically. In that way you come to know not only your dream symbols but you develop an intuitive understanding of their meaning—both for the present and the future. Most of your prophetic dreams will predict your own future. But occasionally events in your future will be newsworthy, such as the following example.

In August 1971, when I was living in New York City but planning to move to San Francisco, I recorded a dream about witnessing a minor earthquake. I published part of the dream with the prediction: 'May be partially precognitive of an earthquake I shall witness one day.... Since I am planning to go to the West Coast, it is more logical for it to be there.'

The rest of the drama described confusion over a commuter train ticket, resolved when a parapsychological colleague, Rex Stanford of Texas, found the ticket. The commuter train ticket seemed odd since I had never used one before.

Soon after I moved to San Francisco in 1973, the Bay Area Rapid Transit (BART), a commuter train, went into operation. A train commuter ticket now became a possibility. When Rex Stanford visited San Francisco on two occasions, I wondered if there would be an earthquake. Then in August 1979 the Parapsychological Association was planning its first Bay Area convention at St Mary's College in Moraga. I was planning to attend and would have to take the BART train. Rex Stanford was planning to attend. This could be it, I thought.

On the opening day of the convention I was asked to appear on a radio program broadcast by KQED, a special series on the mind. The interviewer, Kevin Purseglove, asked me about parapsychological research and concluded his questioning by asking if I had any predictions.

'Just one,' I said. 'I am expecting a small earthquake in the Moraga-Orinda area where the parapsychologists are meeting—because of a dream I had eight years ago. The earthquake will have to be in the next two to three days.'

Two days later, precisely at 8.43 on the morning of 17 August, my San Francisco apartment twisted and jolted as I was dressing to attend the convention.

'Ah!' I exclaimed, 'there's my predicted earthquake.' I wasn't worried about it since my 1971 dream told me it would be minor. As it turned out, the epicenter struck one mile away from the parapsychologists' meeting place in the Moraga-Orinda area.

When I arrived at the convention, one of the first people I talked to was a parapsychologist I had met some months before in New York, Nancy Sondow. She showed me a dream she had recorded about *me*. In her dream I was having problems with a train ticket. I explained that I did indeed have my usual problems with the BART computer train ticket the day before—when she had her dream. I was intrigued because of the connection with my dream of 1971 in which a train ticket assumed so much importance for a time when there would be an earthquake with Rex Stanford around.

By noticing two of the dream's elements about to come into reality, I was able to predict the third element—the earthquake—to complete fulfillment of the eight-year-old dream.

Psychic Househunting

Perhaps the greatest motivation for future sight is insecurity in the present. A situation that lends itself well to such future sight—or call it 'precognitive remote viewing'—is knowing you have to move but not knowing where to. The first time I tried precognitive remote viewing was in 1968 when my first wife and I were living in Utrecht, Holland, and were preparing to move to Freiburg, Germany. Being a university town, Frieburg has a terrible housing shortage. The University placement service was no help at all. So I attempted to picture myself in the future and to describe where I was living. I saw an enormous concrete building in which there was modern furniture. Nearby was a church, a bridge over a river, and a cobbled street.

My wife and I stayed in a hotel while we looked for a place to rent. A few days of house-hunting were fruitless. Finally we saw an advertisement in a newspaper for a room to let. Walking a mile through the rain to the agency, we got the address of the house. It was exactly as I had pictured it. We rented the room. It seemed to be the only one in the town.

In 1981, when living in Los Angeles, my present wife and I were alarmed to hear that our landlord's son was going to move into our rented house. Finding a place for our children and dog would not be easy. I looked into the future to see where we would be living. I saw a two-bedroom house with a fireplace on the left, a porch with square pillars, a fenced-in back yard, an office in the back, and fruit trees. I dowsed on a map of Los Angeles county to find the location: right in the middle of Glendale.

A few weeks later we answered an advertisement for a house for rent in Glendale. I stood in front of the house with my notes and checked off the similarities: everything was there. The landlord later told me that when I and my family walked into the house, it seemed as if we belonged there. I told him that was exactly what I felt but did not go into the reasons why.

Sources of Error

Typically, the raw data of psychic sensing, like dreams, do not contain specific references to future time. Our time sense is located in our left brain hemisphere, but our psychic sense is located in the right. In order to successfully predict time, we must learn how to transfer information back and forth between hemispheres. One helpful technique is to visualize mental calendars for time estimation. Or you might visualize the 12 months of the year as the hours on a clock.

Make your estimated predictions and get feedback. If habitually practiced, time sensing can become second nature. It is important to realize, though, that future events are not frozen in time but shift according to human free will. Some events get postponed, some never happen at all, and some may even be prevented from happening.

The single greatest obstacle to accurate prophecy is excess emotion. If we strongly desire something to happen, our chances of prophetic success diminish. If our emotional desires, wishes, hopes, fantasies enter into our consideration when prophesying, we are only projecting the future the way we want it to be, not what it will be. When emotion is expressed on a negative level, we project our worst fears and nightmares—even feelings of personal dissatisfaction and ill health—onto the world in the guise of prophecy. In my own experience I have found that a balance of great interest and emotional objectivity is the best possible attitude when undertaking a predictive task.

Emotional involvement crowds out cool professionalism when *your* life is the subject of prophecy. It takes a great deal of discipline and work to achieve an objectivity about your own future. I find the best attitude to adopt when foreseeing good things in your own life is: it's fine if it happens, but I won't count on it. I can strive mightily to *make* it happen, both physically and psychically, but I will have no cause for disappointment if it does not work out as well as I hope. Nothing in life—especially prophecy—is ever perfect.

The Psychic Bandwagon Effect

The most infamous source of error in prophecy is what I call the 'Psychic Bandwagon Effect'. The same source of error exists among scientific predictors but they call it 'relying on expert forecasts'. The files of the Central Premonitions Registry are clogged with predictions made by people who have been impressed by prophecies made by some famous psychic or scientist. People climb on the psychic bandwagon and offer additional details of the previsioned effect, usually a calamity of world-shaking significance.

A good example of the Psychic Bandwagon Effect is Paul James's book *California Superquake, 1975–1977?: Scientists, Cayce, Psychics Speak*.[23] Inspired by Jess Stearn's 1968 best-seller on Edgar Cayce, *The Sleeping Prophet*, a small army of psychics and would-be psychics reiterated Cayce's prediction that California would suffer such a great earthquake that it would fall into the sea. James collected their predictions and attempted to pinpoint a date—1975–7—for this calamity. A more recent book by Jeffrey Goodman, *We Are the Earthquake Generation*, uses the same formula to predict a later date.[24]

I believe that these earthquake predictions have absolutely no validity. Once someone—even the very best psychic—has accepted an idea logically, objectivity is lost; the logical mind takes over and masquerades as psychic intuition. For the record, Jess Stearn, who popularized the California superquake thesis, now lives on the coast of Southern California. When asked if he was worried, he replied that he felt the Cayce prediction was about the far future. Cayce's prophecies of cataclysmic shifting of the earth's poles around the beginning of the third millennium first aroused my interest in 1966. Researching other sources of similar predictions for my book *Patterns of Prophecy*, I was struck by the coincidence of these parallel predictions. Taking this research further, author John White has compiled a massive collection of pole shift predictions in his book, *Pole Shift: Predictions and Prophecies of the Ultimate Disaster*.[25] I can discount some of the recent predictions on the grounds of the Psychic Bandwagon Effect, but there remains a residue of prophecy that makes me respectful of the concept, if skeptical of the dates. As I wrote in that book's foreword, 'I, for one, will keep a careful eye out for any fulfilled predictions that are on the psychic timetable to precede the prophesied pole shift.... If there's something to it, we should be finding out sooner than we may like to think.' I feel certain that the conscious minds of these psychics have elaborated, embroidered, exaggerated the prophetic impulses from their deep unconscious, so I dismiss the predicted details.

But a gnawing intuition makes me suspect that a possible trigger for a pole shift—the approach of some celestial body or dark star—may be a real possibility by the century's end or the next millennium's beginning. I feel no need for panic or preparations for catastrophe, but I do feel a need for more acute scientific exploration of our nearby heavens. Something is on its way—something indescribable. It will inspire awe more than terror, wonder more than fear, and have as its greatest impact on the human race a raising of consciousness that will usher in a new era of understanding. Because that statement does not make any logical sense, it must come from the unconscious. It is a prophecy, not a prediction. Perhaps we will soon be in a position to make predictions on a scientific basis about this approaching entity. Even now, astronomers are searching the heavens for evidence of a dark star called 'Nemesis'. In the meanwhile, we have much to learn about the scientific basis of prophecy.

To obtain reliable psychic information about large-scale future events, we must seek out data on the personal level. We must investigate and record dreams and intuitions, must inaugurate scientific study of prophetic impulses of the general populace, study premonitions that happen daily to thousands of people, compare data and fit the peices of the puzzle of the future into place. Each of us foresees imperfectly but together we may glimpse a truer picture of tomorrow's promise—and premonition.

The more abstract an event is, the more difficult it is to predict.

Only by tuning in to individuals who will partake in some future event can we rely on prophetic accuracy. In your experiments in prophecy, do not leap on the psychic bandwagon; do not attempt to predict global disasters and earthquakes. Start with something small, something that interests you, something that you can make psychic contact with but can maintain emotional objectivity about—and above all, something that you can get feedback on soon.

When I studied with Gerard Croiset in Holland, he told me that the psychic information he received then was no better than when he had begun to do psychic work 20 years before, but through intensive study, analysis, and application of logic, he learned to extract far more meaning and accuracy out of his raw psychic data. There is just no substitute for practice, study and discipline. Mastering the art of prophecy is like learning a foreign language: you have 10,000 mistakes to make. The faster you make them, the faster you learn.

Exercises

Dream Prophecy

1. If you have recorded a dream about some person whose future interests you, write out the major elements of the dream and translate them from symbols into basic themes.
2. If you do not already have such a dream, review the Exercise section in 'Training Your Dream Tigers' (Chapter 2) and program a dream about some target person.
3. Does your dream refer to the future or to precognition? Do any of the dream's elements have a prophetic quality? Does the dream describe something that has not happened in the past but conceivably could happen in the future? Briefly describe what your dream might predict.
4. Now try to rule out possible personal references. Ask yourself if the target person might be a symbol for some aspect of yourself. Does the dream remind you of any current situation in your own life? Did you make contact with the target person just before the dream? If the dream does not seem drawn from your own life, and you have been thinking about the target person, assume that your dream may be about that person's experience.
5. If there was a reference to a past event in your dream, assume that your prediction will be fulfilled in about the same distance of time in the future.

6. If your dream seems to predict the near future, and might interest the target person, share your dream with him or her and ask for feedback.

7. If your dream prediction is fulfilled in some way, study the correspondences with what actually happened. This will give you a better idea of how your individual dreaming style previsions the future.

Psychic Prophecy

1. Select as your target some scheduled future event that interests you and involves a target person whose photo is available. You can also make contact with a target person by watching him on television.

2. Touch the photo of the target person or create that person's image in your mind's eye to make psychic contact.

3. Ask your inner self to give you pictures in your mind's eye to show you the future. You may wish to speak your impressions into a tape recorder. Pay attention to images quickly flashing through your mind's eye. Do not attempt to interpret them initially, just observe them. If any words come to mind, record them also. Only after you have established a flow of imagery, sensations and impressions should you try to ask for specific information, such as names, places, and times. Initials are more to be trusted than full names.

4. After your impression session, analyze your images as if they were elements of a dream. Try to translate your impressions into a coherent prediction.

5. In your mind's eye create a calendar of the future and ask when the event might occur.

6. If your prediction seems at variance with what experts think or what you might have guessed, register it with American Prophecy Project, 357 Bowery, New York, NY 10003.

7. When the outcome of the future event becomes known, compare your prediction with details of what happened. Did some of the images you thought were literal turn out to be symbolic? If there is a striking correspondence with your prediction, send a copy of the news item to the American Prophecy Agency.

7.

Personal Dream Prophecy

How far in time are we able to dream about our personal futures? Since 1968 I have been recording dreams to answer that question. My research project began when I was studying in Germany at the institute for Border Areas of Psychology and Mental Health at Freiburg. The institute's director, Hans Bender, introduced me to Christine Mylius, an actress who had been recording her dreams and filing them with the institute for 20 years. About 10 per cent of her dreams proved to be precognitive. Some of these precognitive dreams were prophetic of movie roles she played years later, about which Bender made a documentary film.

Inspired by Christine Mylius, I began to record my own dreams with the intention of dreaming about the future. One of my first prophetic dreams foretold the assassination of Robert Kennedy. I had registered this dream premonition with parapsychologist Stanley Krippner at the Maimonides Dream Laboratory in Brooklyn.

In 1969 I moved to Brooklyn and Krippner invited me to become a subject in dream-telepathy experiments for two years. Some of these experimentally recorded dreams turned out to be precognitive of events in my own life. The fulfillment of one intriguing dream took place at the Dream Lab. in an unofficial experiment filmed for Canadian television.

Here is the dream of 3 April 1969, which I pointed out on 17 July to Dr Montague Ullman, the Director of the Dream Lab, as possibly being precognitive of a future experiment at the lab. The experimenter was Charles Honorton.

Fifth Dream Report: Chuck [Honorton] was looking over a report of some previous experiment, and he had marked for some reason through the transcript 'F's which meant failures.... There was a television set in the room ... as I was looking at it, I watched a scene. There was a man with a knife in his hand and out in a corner was outstretched a monkey....

Post-Sleep Interview: I was lying in bed and Chuck Honorton was there and he was marking a transcript and he was using the letter 'F' as a symbol for something.... He said, 'Oh, 'F' is for failure.' Then I looked at the television set there and this television set actually seemed to be part of the experiment as well ... as I looked at it, the whole thing began to move and come to life, and there was a man holding a knife ... and behind him was a monkey lying on the floor, and there may have been someone else there as well.... I wonder if there might be sometime an experimental thing like this....

On 12 January 1970—nine months later—the Canadian television personality Norman Perry arrived at the Dream Laboratory to film an experiment for Canadian TV. Perry was to be the dream subject, and I was to be a back-up subject in case he couldn't get to sleep or remember dreams. A target pool of pictures had been made up the day before, and that night the agent, Don Rice, was in another building looking at the randomly selected target pictures. Charles Honorton was the experimenter.

In the morning, after Perry's and my dreams were recorded, the target pool of pictures was brought in and we made our judgings from the experimenter's notes. I judged a miss. It turned out that my dreams were only about the agent's associations with the target, and not about the target itself. Perry, however, scored a direct hit. Since I was there only as a back-up subject, it was decided to film Perry's judgings alone.

As the cameras for the TV show went into action, I watched the scene. Several other persons watched as well. Perry put the oversized target pictures on the floor and pointed out his first choice: a photo of an albino monkey. This corresponded with his dream image of a white animal and the strikingly correct detail of a blue broadloom rug. Perry then pointed out this second choice: a man holding an axe.

The correspondences between my dream and the actual events are:

1. I was lying in bed (as a subject for a dream experiment).
2. Charles Honorton was there.
3. A transcript from a previous experiment (that of 3 April 1969) was pertinent.
4. My judging was a failure.

5. I watched the scene.
6. Instead of a television set, there were cameras for television.
7. There was a 'monkey' lying on the floor.
8. Instead of a man holding a knife, there was a man holding an axe.
9. There were other people present.
10. It was 'an experimental thing'.

It may be that the unusual excitement of a television filming singled out in my unconscious that particular experiment to dream about nine months before it took place. Moreover, I had been attempting to document precognition in an irrefutable way. Thus a unique opportunity was offered not only to record on tape the dream itself but also to film its fulfillment. One reason for singling out that dream as precognitive of a future experiment at the Dream Lab. was, of course, that the setting was the Dream Laboratory. Another was the appearance of a television set. At that time I did not even own a television set, so it seemed an odd thing to dream about. The dream precognitively focused on an event of more than usual interest, since during the course of the experiment I was invited by Norman Perry to appear on his nationwide show in Canada to discuss precognitive dreams the following October.

Television was again the theme of a dream I recorded at home in Brooklyn on 12 December 1968. The dream began:

> I was working in an office with two women. We were working late. I was called away for a television interview, with another woman. Together, we discussed the behaviour of another woman TV personality, with me defending her. I didn't see any cameras but somehow I knew that I was on TV. I was surprised to feel so relaxed and self-assured, and I thought I put my case very well. Then I returned to my office.... I wonder if indeed I shall be interviewed on TV some day, as this is the second dream about it.

Nearly nine years later, on 26 April 1977, I was working in San Francisco at *Psychic* magazine, sharing an office with two women. Gayle Delaney, a dream-psychologist friend, arranged for me to appear with her on an hour-long show to be taped that day for Channel 2 (KTVU) in Oakland. Delaney drove to my office, picked me up, and took me to the taping. The topic of discussion was dreams. The interviewer, Julie Yip, was both charming and intelligent in her questions about Delaney's technique for 'incubating dreams'—asking the unconscious for a dream to solve a specific problem. I defended Delaney's technique with my own examples of dream incubation—asking for dreams about the future. I told them about my 1968 dream of being on television with them. I thought that Delaney made an excellent TV personality, with or without my defending her. She went on to do many TV shows. As in the dream, I didn't see any cameras because I was turned to face the interviewer. As in my dream, I felt relaxed and self-assured. And, as in the dream, I returned to the office.

By now I have been on television over 50 times, but this was one of the few shows devoted exclusively to dreams—hence, perhaps, my prophetic dream about it.

Yet another television show was predicted in a dream of 1 June 1977, when living in San Francisco. In the dream people said they had been watching me on TV and wondered where I had taped an appearance. 'It was in San Rafael,' I replied. My comment on this was, 'Perhaps a TV series will be shaping up ... and have something to do with someone living in San Rafael.'

On 19 July 1987, now living in Los Angeles, I was invited to visit Dr Jeffrey Mishlove in San Rafael in Northern California to tape a TV show for his new TV series titled *Thinking Allowed*. The series is now being shown on PBS and is available on videocasette from Spectrum Foundation. Mishlove lived in San Francisco at the time of the dream over 10 years before.

This next dream occurred on 18 March 1970, when I was living in Brooklyn:

> I was answering an advertisement for editorial work. A young woman answered the door and showed me a newsletter—connected with astrology or occult things—that she needed help with. She invited me in and there I met several other young women. I started chatting with one, when a large black dog came up to us and appeared to be eating an address someone had written out. The dog's name was Tiny Tim.

In October 1982, while living in Los Angeles, I did answer a newspaper advertisement for editorial work. I got the job as editor of *Reincarnation Report*, which has run articles on astrology and other 'occult' things.

When I arrived at my new office in Malibu, I was introduced to several young women working there. I had an office mate, Christine Conrad, who was sitting on the floor and assembling stacks of catalog mailouts. A powerful sense of *déjà vu* came over me. 'I've seen you before,' I said. 'It must have been in a dream a long time ago. In the dream you had a large black dog named Tiny Tim.'

'I do have a large black dog,' replied Christine, 'but I'm the one who is Tiny Tim. That was my first and only stage role.'

That evening I went through my dream diary to find the Tiny Tim dream. The next day I discussed it with the publisher of *Reincarnation Report*, Dick Sutphen. In 1970 he had no inkling of plans to move from Arizona to Malibu to start a magazine. An elaborate series of events had led to Christine's employment in the office. The black dog wasn't even born then. Were our lives already set up in blueprint form 12 years before?

The question extended to 16 years when I recently reviewed some transcripts of psychic dream experiments done at Maimonides Dream Laboratory in 1969. For several years after the 1969 experiments I would occasionally review the dream records and puzzle over what this dream could possibly mean. It was triggered by a friend who mentioned before the experiment that she had just read Philip Roth's novel *Goodbye, Columbus.*

On 28 March 1969, my sixth dream report, as told to Stanley Krippner and transcribed for record was (edited verbatim from four pages):

I was walking back from a mess hall, and music was playing—something to do with Columbus.... It seemed to be after the experiment, or even before the experiment was quite over, and I talked there with some people who I had known before. I talked in particular to this one chap I seemed to have known before. He said he was going to go to Erin on the weekend ... he spoke of flying to Erin ... it's Ireland.... He had to carry some sort of equipment along with him so he could function all right....

I remember now the reason I left this mess hall was because the food was so bad that I decided that I'd have to go out and find something to eat....

The person about whom I was giving this reading ... may have been Negro....

And I was walking up steps and they were very peculiar steps because the water was coursing down them and each step was like a little pool... And coming down from this were a group of children.... I had to stop along the side in order to let them pass by, and it was at this point that I was hearing the song about Columbus....

The name of Columbus immediately brought to mind an ESP experiment in which I participated with the Mobius Society in

1985. In March of that year marine archaeologist Roger C. Smith telephoned Mobius Society director Stephan Schwartz for help in locating two lost ships of Columbus in St Ann's Bay in Jamaica. The caravels had been missing for nearly five centuries. Schwartz agreed to undertake an experiment in collaboration with Smith. In August 1985 Stephan Schwartz, Rand De Mattei and I, along with two other Mobius consultants, flew from Los Angeles to Jamaica. We stayed in a small hotel next to the archaeologists' residence, which also served as a mess hall.

The 'chap I seemed to have known before' was Stephan Schwartz. Earlier he had to fly to Ireland to work on a case of a kidnapped horse. The equipment that my dream saw him wearing 'so he could function all right' turned out to be oxygen tanks for functioning underwater.

The mess hall with the bad food was only too real. It was not the fault of our cook but of the budget: 35 dollars a week to feed a dozen people. We went out to eat several times.

The most unusual event in our Columbus mission was a visit to Dunn's Falls, an amazing waterfall that cascades down dozens of natural stone steps, each step forming a pool of water. It took more than an hour for our group to climb up the steps. At one point we had to stop along the side to let a group of children come down. I was helped up the slippery steps by our cook's assistant, a young black man for whom I had, in fact, given a psychic reading. Our 'hydrological experience,' as Smith termed it, came at the end of our two-week visit. We were saying, 'Goodbye, Columbus.' (The experiment itself is described in the next chapter.)

Now a skeptic might say that just by chance I should eventually over the years experience a combination of *Columbus, an ESP experiment, a mess hall with bad food, a friend who flew to Ireland and who wore strange equipment, climbing up the steps of an unusual waterfall, and a black man for whom I did a reading.* Yet I find that skeptical explanation hard to believe. Such a highly specific combination of unusual life events seems to rule out chance correspondence. And so, I ask, were we all (Smith, Schwartz, De Mattei and the others) participating in a joint life plan?

A recent Mobius project of searching for a sunken treasure-ship also seemed forecast by dreams. The first voyage of the Mobius research vessel *Seaview* in September 1987 from Ft Lauderdale, Florida, seemed to be forecast in a dream I recorded on 21 March 1986:

Visiting in Florida

I was about to leave from a visit. I was walking towards an old brick building on the water. I passed a group of people I seemed to know and waved to them. I told them I would be back in a little bit to say goodbye. Among them was Fran, who lives in Florida....

I commented: 'I wonder if the dream could be symbolic of my working with a group in Florida?'

Eighteen months later (September 1987), Mobius flew me to Ft Lauderdale to join a group abroad the *Seaview*. The 125-foot ship was docked near an old red brick building. We stayed in dock for a few days and then went to the Bahamas in search of sunken ships. When we sailed back to Ft Lauderdale, I was one of the first people off the boat, as I had only a short time to catch the last airplane back to Los Angeles. I said goodbye to the group and promised to return soon. I learned that Fran had in fact been invited but was unable to join us.

The second voyage of *Seaview* seemed to turn up in a dream I had recorded nearly 11 years before (10 June 1977):

The Ocean Voyage

I was coming back on an ocean liner. We were soon to dock so I cleaned my gear out of my locker. I had not yet paid for my return ticket so I tried to find the office to pay.... Meanwhile I talked with some other people. We were learning Portuguese. I think we were headed for South America.

On 2 May 1988 I was coming back from a week's voyage on the *Seaview*. I cleaned out my locker and packed. I talked with the cook, Gabrielle Silva, who said that she was learning Portuguese in preparation for going to South America (Brazil) to work on an educational project. I had to get additional funds from Mobius for my return air ticket from Miami, since cancelled flights from the Bahamas had made me miss my scheduled flight and I did not have a reservation. But, luckily, I was able to talk my way out of paying more. The return from an ocean voyage with someone who is learning Portuguese and going to South America, coupled with concern for paying for the return trip, seemed unlikely to have occurred by chance.

Many of my prophetic dreams forecast times of major career events. Of 222 dreams recorded at home between 1968 and 1977, I count 63 as precognitive (28 per cent) and add seven more that were recorded in the Dream Lab, making a total of 70 precognitive dreams from that period. (The cutoff date was forced on me when a later dream diary was stolen from the car of a television producer.) The dream-event correspondences tend to show a clustering around major transition points in my life. I noticed such a clustering in spring 1988 when seven precognitive dreams described events associated with the major career commitment of starting a computer software company. The dreams dated from 1969, 1970, 1973, 1976 and 1977. Here are a few examples.

A second dream of the Dream Lab. on 18 March 1969, reported just before the 'Goodbye, Columbus' dream, referred to 'Fortune-Telling Dials' and an oil can labeled 'Lubricant for Fortune-Telling Dials'. The 'Fortune-Telling Dial' is an excellent description of 'Psychic Reward', a computerized intuition training system that I am working on. I call it 'an electronic wheel of fortune'. On 7 March 1988, after reviewing the dream, I studied a printout of the Psychic Reward design and wondered how on earth it might be related to an oil can. My wife arrived and said that she had taken the car in for a 'lube' job at Oil Can Henry's, and showed me the invoice. About that time, my collaborator on Psychic Reward, Jack Houck, called to tell me he had 'swatted some bugs' in the program—was 'lubricating' the 'Fortune-Telling Dial' to make it run better. So the oil can and the Fortune-Telling Dial finally came together—after 19 years.

On the morning of 18 March I experienced a strong sense of *déjà vu* when I took the cover off my electric typewriter. Brazenly poised there was a cockroach. I attempted to swat it but inadvertantly dropped it into the machine's innards. I was wondering how to get it out when I remembered that I once had a dream about cockroaches. I found the dream report dated 4 April 1973: I had dreamed about holding a cockroach with tweezers and attempting to put it on repro proofs I was correcting. The dream gave me the idea of using tweezers to remove the cockroach, but I still couldn't locate it. Later that day I was correcting repro proofs for a flyer.

On that same day I contracted for a new office for my newly formed software company, Mind Technology Systems. Again, I experienced a sense of *déjà vu* as I noted that the office was a bungalow with a fireplace, and had a patio-garden with round tables and chairs. Going through my dream records, I found a dream of 24 April 1969 which described the new office: a bungalow with a patio-garden and round tables and chairs. The dream's association was to a psychic prediction about having a fireplace. It all finally happened 19 years later—a pivotal time in my life. I was considering moving to Malibu but decided instead to stay in the same neighbourhood and rent a larger office.

My decision *not* to move to a house in Malibu was made largely on the strength of a recent dream, in which I was in the new house and making out a check for the rent. A shark threw itself against the door and forced it open. I shut the door, and again the shark thudded against it. My analysis was: 'Wolves at the door are bad enough, but sharks really mean nasty business. Don't take the house.' So I rejected the possible future shown in the shark dream, but choose instead the possible future I had dreamed about 19 years before.

One of my most remarkable long-term dream prophecies was recently fulfilled after more than 16 years. On 30 September 1973 I dreamed about a haunted hotel:

> With a group of people I went to work for a short while in a haunted hotel.... Sure enough the ghost is there, a woman ghost.
>   Then I was on some sort of TV entertainment show.... The Emcee, a man, gives me his credit card to use ... at the bar. At the bar, I am talking to a very attractive woman in French.... She wants me to appear on a TV show (she is apparently a producer).

At the time of the dream in 1973, I met an attractive TV producer whose name was Mary Jo French, which stimulated my subconscious to dream about a future meeting on 15 February 1990, with another attractive TV producer, whose first name is French—Renée Kenneth, a producer with the syndicated TV show *After Hours*. She invited me to appear on the show to discuss ghosts at the *Queen Mary*, which is now a hotel docked permanently at Long Beach. Strangely, we were videotaped in the bar, where indeed the Emcee, a man, bought me a drink. I was debating, with a skeptical physicist about ghosts—such as the female ghost seen on the *Queen Mary*. Millions of television viewers were witness to the fulfillment of my dream. Renée Kenneth's reaction to my prophetic dream was, 'That's spooky.' I concede it upsets the arguments of skeptical physicists.

My dream odyssey through time continues. For me it was a great surprise to find that events many years in the future could be accurately dreamt about. When I began my experiment, I supposed that events near in time would be easier to dream about than events far in time, and in fact, physicist Russell Targ has made such an experimental prediction. Yet the detailed correspondences of the 'Goodbye, Columbus' and 'Haunted Hotel' dreams, both fulfilled after more than 16 years, shattered that concept.

I do not feel that these prophetic dreams predict the only future. Many other dreams, unfulfilled, may well describe alternate futures that were not realized because of my choices of free will. We'll never know for sure. But certainly the precognitive dreams recorded here strongly suggest that major events in one's personal future are determined in blueprint form many years before. It was up to me, and many others, to make those blueprints become reality.

Exercise

Reviewing your Dream Diary
1. Periodically review your dream diary to look for correspondences with later events—especially emotionally significant events.
2. Look for thematic statements in your dreams that might parallel later real-life events.
3. Look for unusual situations in your dreams that correspond with present events. Two or more unusual corresponding items are significant.
4. Be alert to symbolic substitutions in your dreams. Your associations at the time of the dream may connect with the later event.
5. Keep a record of dream-event correspondences in your dream diary. How far in time have your dreams predicted your future?

8.

Making Prophecy Practical

The skeptic's classic question is, 'If you're so psychic, why aren't you rich?'

If you could foresee the future, couldn't you make money by gambling or on the financial markets? Although some people have had occasional success with intuitive predictions about horse races and gambling, their abilities tend to fall away once they fall victim to the impulse of greed. I believe the main problem in trying to use psychic abilities in a gambling situation is the 'I win, you lose' situation. Even worse, the money is not put to work; it just changes pockets.

When Israeli psychic Uri Geller first visited the United States, he tried gambling in Las Vegas casinos. He lost heavily. He should be grateful he did. If he had won, he might have been tempted to make gambling his life's work and would still be in Vegas. Instead, he moved to England and for the past 10 years has been working in 'win, win' situations for mining companies. Geller gets a tiny percentage of profits from locating new mineral deposits, such as gold. Geller wins only if his clients win. Something useful comes out *if*. And the rewards for Geller have been considerable: he has made over 40 million dollars. Skeptics of Geller's psychic ability have a hard time explaining that away.

People are forever asking me to predict winning lottery numbers for them and to give them other assistance in obtaining quick money without work. I patiently explain that their life path is not to sit on their behinds and count cash.

Moreover, if the legendary Man Who Broke the Bank at Monte Carlo is any example, quick cash is not necessarily the answer. At his last visit to Monte Carlo in 1891, Englishman Charles Wells went to a roulette table and let his money ride on 5. The number 5 came up 5 times in a row. Beating odds of 69 million to 1, Wells took away 98,000 francs. He lost it all in dubious speculations and died broke in prison.

Could the future be foreseen with perfect accuracy? And if so, would we want to? If the future could be perfectly foreseen, that future would have to be 100 per cent predetermined. So no matter what we do, we could not change such a predetermined future. It would truly be, *que sera, sera* — 'What will be, will be.' In fact, there would be little point in attempting to look into the future. In a universe that had only one future, we could never hope. For better — and mostly, worse — we would always know. We would never attempt difficult challenges if we knew that sure failure lay ahead. And so we would not get the experience that finally leads to success. A completely predetermined universe would rob us of our most precious gift — free will.

Fortunately, there is no evidence that the future can be completely foreseen. The highest scoring precognition laboratory subject I know of is the Englishman Malcolm Bessent. In 16 attempts to dream about future picture targets at the Maimonides Dream Lab., Bessent was successful in 14 of them, giving him a success rate of 87.5 per cent. An important ingredient in Bessent's success, I feel, was the 'win-win' atmosphere at the Maimonides Lab. All the research personnel wanted him to succeed. He did not have to buck skeptical antagonism, neither was there any competition.

How does the accuracy of precognition compare with present-time ESP? One widely circulated statement says that Edgar Cayce was 85 per cent accurate in his predictions. A more accurate statement would be that out of the 50 per cent of people who responded to a questionnaire about Cayce's readings for them, 85 per cent said they found the readings helpful. Since Cayce's readings were primarily medical in nature, that statistic is meaningful. The survey did not attempt to answer the question of how accurate Cayce's *predictions* were.[25]

As to the famous earth-change predictions made by Cayce, Mark Thurston, the research director of the ARE (Association for Research and Enlightenment, founded by Cayce), could not find a single fulfillment. 'We have no solid evidence for Cayce's skill at predicting earth changes,' comments Thurston.[28] One theory to account for this inaccuracy is that 50 years ago Cayce was predicting events which were then in the blueprint stage but which subsequently were changed. This is the theory I favor.

In my own experience in real-life situations, the accuracy of present-time ESP can reach a 100 per cent under the right conditions. For example, when a family asked me to locate their stolen antique car, I described a specific location in Los Angeles and pinpointed it on a map. I described two youths who had taken the car to a garage and were painting it white. I told the family that if they went immediately to the location they might be lucky and find the car. I cautioned them that the youths were planning to ship the car out of state soon.

That evening the family went to my described location and reported to me that their car was being painted white by the two thieves in the garage I had described. They were indeed lucky in finding it, but as it turned out, they could not convince a policeman to go into that dangerous area to arrest the youths. When the family finally persuaded a police officer to investigate, the car was gone. If that story has a moral, it is that even perfect ESP will not necessarily solve your problem.

Consensus Predictions

One of the most powerful tools for enhancing the accuracy of precognition is finding consensus among independent psychic sources. In 1967 I began collecting predictions from British psychics and mediums. Mostly their predictions were about me. I found consensus in several of their predictions which were, in fact, fulfilled. A dozen said I would work in psychic matters myself. Seven predicted I would write books. Six predicted I would lecture. Five predicted I would move to California. Two predicted I would work with a psychic magazine.

In the seven years it took to get my first book published, I often reviewed the predictions to give me moral strength. The odds of getting a book manuscript published are 100 to 1. So it took a lot of doing on my part to fulfill the consensus predictions.

One of the strongest consensus themes was for a period more than 20 years later (i.e. now). Eight psychics predicted I would have something to do with writing for movies, television or the stage. A film and TV project are now in the works.

In December 1976 I help set up an experiment to test the validity of consensus predictions. Living in San Francisco at the time, I proposed to the *San Francisco Chronicle* that they run a group of predictions made in response to the same questions. A reporter, Steve Rubenstein, asked five yes/no questions about the burning issues he saw for 1977:

- Will there be a big earthquake?
- Will President Carter be assassinated?
- Will Patty Hearst be in jail?
- Will California Governor Jerry Brown be married?
- Who will be the Superbowl winner, Oakland or Minnesota?

Two additional questions called for number estimates: What will be the Dow-Jones Industrials average on 31 January 1977? In what place will the San Francisco Giants finish in 1977?

Predictions were made by myself and five other Bay Area psychics: Frank Nocerino, Jeanne Borgen, Macelle Brown, Michael Symonds and Shirley Dicker. The mechanical Fortune-telling Grandma at the arcade on Fisherman's Wharf was added as a 'control psychic'. The predictions were published on 1 January 1977, and a followup story was published 2 January 1978.[27] Not every question was answered by all psychics, and in a couple of instances, two responses were given for a single question.

The Table of Predictions for 1977 shows startling correlations. On the yes/no questions, the best that any psychic did individually was four out of five correct (80 per cent); *Consensus gave a stunning 100 per cent correct for all five questions*.

Individual answers to the place in which the Giants would finish were all incorrect. *But the consensus average of fourth place was right.*

Individual answers to the Dow-Jones prediction ranged from 990 (off by 4 per cent from the actual outcome of 954) to 750 (off by 21 per cent) to a consensus average of 869 (off 9 per cent. Getting within 9 per cent of the actual figure seems reasonably good, especially when compared with Grandma.

The Grandma (control psychic) got three out of five correct (60 per cent) of the yes/no questions, wrongly predicted third place for the Giants, and was completely out of the Arcade with Dow-Jones predictions of 44 or 6,302.

The consensus experiment was a stunning success.

In contrast, several Bay Area psychics, including myself, participated in an Earthquake Prediction Panel in 1976 at the World of the Unexplained Museum. All of the other psychics predicted catastrophic earthquakes for San Francisco within a few years. I was the lone holdout, insisting that San Francisco had nothing to worry about for at least 10 years. I was proven correct. But would not a consensus have predicted a catastrophic earthquake? Here we have to watch out for 'The Psychic

Table of Predictions for 1977

Question	Vaughan	Nocerino	Borgen	Brown	Symonds	Dicker	Consensus	Outcome
Big Earthquake?	No	No	No	No	—	No	No	No
Carter Assassinated?	No	Yes	No	—	No	No	No	No
Hearst in Jail?	No	—	Yes	Yes	No	No	No	No
Superbowl Winner?	Minn.	Oak.	Minn.	Oak.	Oak.	—	Oak.	Oak.
Brown Married?	No	No	No	No	No	No	No	No
Giants Finish?	3rd	3rd	—	1st/2nd	—	9th	4th	4th
Dow-Jones on 31 Jan.?	990	750	—	850/857	876/890	—	869	954

Bandwagon Effect'. Once a famous psychic has predicted something, others tend to repeat the prediction. Widely publicized earthquake predictions generated 'psychic noise', which accounted for the false consensus.

Similar 'false consensus' effects were seen in 1975 predictions made by many psychics that President Ford would not complete his term in office. Several specified he would be assassinated. I spotted the 'Psychic Bandwagon Effect' immediately, and in my analysis of the predictions for *Psychic* magazine, scaled it down to conclude: 'By a considerable consensus (13 to 1) the psychics vote that Ford will not be re-elected in 1976.' That proved to be true.[28]

In the laboratory the accuracy rate of consensus predictions has been teased into high above-chance scoring. A problem that has beset parapsychology for years is that some people consistently score below chance—use their ESP to avoid the target. James Carpenter at the University of North Carolina used this to his advantage in experiments with nine groups of students. Carpenter simply sampled their scoring on yes/no targets and reversed their predictions if they tended to score below chance. Students who scored above chance kept their positive predictions. Each student made a number of predictions for the same targets, and the majority vote or consensus was taken as the final prediction. Out of 105 consensus predictions, 80 proved correct—giving a 76 per cent accuracy rate.[29]

In Carpenter's first experiment, the individual success rate was 54 per cent but the majority consensus reached a high of 85 per cent accuracy. If such theoretical accuracy could be translated into the real world, it would make a casino owner tremble.

Consensus Predictions in Archaeology

When there is little or no logical base for predictions and yet a strong consensus emerges from several individuals, we may have a highly reliable predictive tool.

Methods for developing consensus predictions are now being practiced by the Mobius Society in Los Angeles. The first experiments in the practical use of consensus techniques—what I call 'consciousness technology'—enlisted several trained psychics to describe independently where unknown objects might be found and what they looked like. When a group of psychics picked a precise location on sea charts for an unknown shipwreck and described it, Mobius acquired a submarine to dive in the coastal waters off Catalina Island to check out the predictions. A filmed record of stunning success, including several unusual objects described in the predictions and found near the ship, was shown on the series *In Search Of.*

Taking two trained psychics to Egypt, Stephan Schwartz, the director of Mobius, asked them to pinpoint some underground target at a site named Marea. One psychic staked out the outlines of a predicted Byzantine house. When the other psychic was brought in, she confirmed much of what the first psychic said and added some unusual details. An Egyptian archaeologist dismissed their predictions as sheer fantasy. He knew that a magnetometer survey of that area showed nothing.

The dispute was put to test by digging. To the archaeologist's consternation, he found the Byzantine house complete with the predicted details. The stakes were off by about two feet. As Schwartz said in a 1981 presentation to the Parapsychological Association, 'There was no need for statistical evaluation—either you find it or you don't.'

Other successful archaeological finds by Mobius include the remains of the lighthouse of Pharos in the Eastern Harbor of Alexandria, Egypt, the palace of Anthony, and what may be the palace of Cleopatra. The full story is told by Stephen Schwartz in *The Alexandria Project.*[30]

The Psychic Search for Columbus

The psychic search for Columbus began in March 1985 when Stephan Schwartz received a telephone call from marine archaeologist Roger C. Smith. Smith and his team from the Institute of Nautical Archaeology, College Station, Texas, had been searching for Columbus's two lost ships on the shores of St Ann's Bay in Jamaica for four years without success.

When last seen in 1504, the two caravels, named the *Santiago* and *Capitana*, were beached at St Ann's Bay. The ships were in sad condition, wormy and filled with water. Their crew of a hundred had been marooned on the upper decks for a year. Christopher Columbus was thankful to be rescued from this, his fourth voyage, and never again returned to the New World.

Smith asked Schwartz if the Mobius team of intuitives could help him locate the lost caravels.

Working from Los Angeles, I was one of eight intuitive consultants who attempted to describe the caravels and their locations 3,000 miles away in the Caribbean. We were told only the names of Columbus's ships and were asked to pinpoint locations on a map of St Ann's Bay. I marked two locations on land. Two consensus areas emerged from all our location choices: both were in the waters of the bay. We made over a thousand intuitive statements about the lost ships and the terrain, and even about Roger Smith. Of the 445 statements that Smith could evaluate, a remarkable 73 per cent were 'hits' that is, correct and partially correct. The top scorer had a 89 per cent hit rate and I was next at 86 per cent. Not bad, considering none of us knew anything about the ships at St Ann's Bay.

The project got really interesting when three of us intuitives (myself, photographer John Oligny and musician Andre Vaillancourt) and two Mobius researchers, Stephan Schwartz and Rand De Mattei, journeyed to St Ann's Bay to work with the archaeological team in field-testing our hypotheses. We stayed at a little hotel on the bay next to the house rented by the five archaeologists.

Using Mobius's long-standing methodology, we worked together to put the intuitive statements into categories so that similar items could be compared. Finally, Smith revealed to us that the ships had been grounded on the shore and that was where he had searched most intensively. The Mobius personnel developed the intuitive hypothesis that the beached ships had been inundated by earthquake tidal waves and that the ships' superstructures had been swept out into the bay. In fact, as Smith later determined, there were five such tidal waves churned up within six hours by massive earthquakes in 1692. The identifying ballast rocks would remain on shore. But where?

Andre and I felt that the ship locations had been near one of my marks on the map. That was under a modern highway running along the coast. Behind the highway was a field, with 20 feet of boulders filling in beneath. Our one hope for coring was in the earthen floor of a nearby ancient warehouse, which was still in use as an auto repair garage. The owner told us we could core a hole in the floor. But the next day, when we arrived with the equipment, we were denied permission. Perhaps the auto repairman figured out why we wanted to core there. If we found something, his place of business might be turned into a national Columbus shrine.

Smith and his crew of divers searched the bay's waters for debris. They did find old pieces of wood but were unable to identify them. They also found an unknown wreck, specifically described by the intuitives, in our primary consensus area. They found absolutely nothing in other parts of the bay. I was delighted to hear that they found a metal anchor that I had indicated. That find was significant since the magnetomer survey of the area had not revealed it, though intuitive sensing had. The complete report was recently issued by Mobius under the title: *The Caravel Project: Final Report.*[31]

The dramatic story of Columbus's enforced stay on Jamaica was revealed to us as Smith took us to the site where 50 mutineers had set up a camp fortified by a circle of pallisades. This site was close to another location I had marked on the map. Smith told us of the battle that had taken place there. When news arrived that rescue was imminent, Columbus's brother led a group of men to take supplies to the mutineers and was prepared to offer them a pardon. The mutineers, led by two brothers named Porras, attacked them. As amazed Indians watched, the Columbus contigent subdued the mutineers, killing and wounding a few men. They put one of the Porras brothers in irons, and the other mutineers submitted. The united crew was finally rescued on 29 June 1504, after their stay of a year and five days. The story of this voyage was later written by Columbus's son, then a 12-year-old cabin boy.

We were also asked to comment on other archaeological sites. Perhaps the most interesting was a British site that archaeologists had only just started to unearth. I described a sunken ship used as landfill, a wharf area, an adjoining road that slanted so that barrels could be rolled down, and nearby shops. Smith indicated that my description tallied with recently discovered facts that only he knew.

Our psychic search for Columbus was both fascinating and frustrating. Fascinating because we were able to probe the veil of archaeological history with tantalizing clues. Frustrating because so many of the intuitive impressions could not be confirmed one way or the other. Archaeology simply could not answer some of the questions. It would take massive funding to drill through the roadway area to investigate the site below for ballast rocks and other clues, such as a glassy circle of sand where I had psychically seen a forge set up. The pieces of old wood that the divers found cannot be positively identified as belonging to any one ship. Their identity will remain an enigma.

Yet, since such a high percentage of our intuitive statements that could be evaluated did prove to be 'hits' (73 per cent), it seems reasonable that we were probably on target with the others.

The Mobius teamwork approach proved to be highly reliable—more reliable than the statements of any one person. I was quite fascinated to see how several of us would pick up apparently conflicting pieces of the puzzle and how they began to fit together as the story developed. A strong concensus would emerge. An important point is that we were not picking our data up telepathically from Smith since he had an entirely different concept.

Paradoxically, I had predicted at the beginning of the project that nothing of the Columbus ships could be found at this time. Yet it seemed a worthwhile project to undertake. Perhaps as we near the five hundredth anniversary of Columbus's discovery of America in 1992, funds will become available for a definitive archaeological project in Jamaica.

I believe the most important finding from our Columbus mission was in refining the methodology for converting intuitive impressions into reliable data.

Exercise

What will be in the Microwave?
This is the same game as before, with the difference that the subjects are asked to intuitively predict what *will* be in the microwave.

1. One person plays the role of experimenter and selects pairs of household objects that are different from each other, say a banana and a salt shaker. The experimenter assembles the objects in the kitchen and makes certain that the subjects do not see the objects.
2. The subjects go to the living room or some other room not adjacent to the kitchen. They have paper and pens.
3. The experimenter goes to the subjects and tells them, 'You are going out of your body and forward in time a few minutes. You will go into the kitchen and look at whatever object will be in the microwave in three minutes. Draw what you see.' The experimenter goes to the kitchen.
4. The subjects make drawings of their mental perceptions.
5. The experimenter then flips a coin to determine which of two paired objects will be the target. He puts the target in the microwave.
6. After a few minutes the experimenter removes the target object from the microwave. He takes it to the subjects and asks, 'Is

this what you saw in the microwave?'
7. The subjects compare their drawings with the target object.
    They look for consensus in their drawings.
8. The experimenter then brings in the control object of the pair
    and the subjects compare their drawings with the control
    object.

Hints for Intuitive Prediction

Here are some hints for enhancing your powers of intuitive
prediction:

1. Doubt everything you think you know about a certain
    situation, person, or future event. Assume the experts might be
    wrong. Make your mind truly open. Assume a playful attitude.
2. Word the question so that the answer can be seen as a mental
    picture. If the question is a simple yes/no type, ask to see some
    symbol of that.
3. While you are seeing the mental pictures do not attempt to
    analyze their meaning, but merely record what you see. After
    you have finished with your mental imagery, then you can ask
    for their meaning.
4. Pay attention to feelings in your solar plexus that accompany
    your images. A relaxed, warm feeling means 'yes'; a tight,
    anxious feeling means 'no'.
5. Practice getting answers to the small questions in life before
    trusting the answers to the big questions. The more you use
    your intuition, the more you will come to rely on it.
6. Ask others for their intuitive hunches about your questions—
    especially if they have no knowledge of present circumstances.
    Look for consensus. And remember: intuition rushes in where
    logic fears to tread.

9.

The Science of Prediction

Scientific forecasting pervades every aspect of our lives and spawns several multi-billion dollar industries. It is an accepted fact in our technological society that scientific experts should be able to make the most accurate predictions about the future. Indeed, they are handsomely paid to do so. Experts in weather forecasting, finance, economics, politics, business, and so on, build computerized models of the future extrapolated from the past and present. The media are full of their predictions. But there is seldom any follow-up to judge their accuracy.

Just how successful is scientific forecasting? The answers may surprise you.

Weather Forecasting

The National Weather Service of the United States boasts multi-million dollar satellites and sophisticated computers to arrive at their weather forecasts. At Massachusetts Institute of Technology, Dr Frederick Sanders, a professor of meterology, has been keeping an eye on the weathermen. His verdict: 'Our skill in forecasting tomorrow's weather has apparently *decreased* slightly in the past 20 years.'[32]

Dr Sanders puts the blame on too great a reliance on computers. The human factor—call it 'judgement' or 'intuition'—is better at prediction than computers.

The computerized forecasts are 80 per cent accurate in predicting rain for the next day. But after that accuracy falls dramatically, with fourth-day forecasts being no better than chance.

Stock Market Prediction

'I describe its performance as like the unpredictable, mindless ramblings of a drunk,' says Dr Kosaku Yoshida, professor of finance at California State University. In his 20-year study of the market, he has used computers to check out various theories and professional strategies for predicting the market.[33] They all give results no better than chance. Several studies found no difference when comparing stocks picks made by professional financial analysts with stocks picked at chance. They did equally as well or equally as badly.

In a study of the 20 top financial analysts made by *Financial World*, the highly paid (100–200,000 dollars a year) experts 'bombed out on two-thirds of their stock picks.'[34]

A survey of stock prediction studies since 1900 was made by J. Scott Armstrong, an associate professor at the Wharton School, University of Pennsylvania. Surprisingly, he found no significant advantage for logical expertise. For example, a highly touted *Wall Street Journal* columnist made 90 predictions of the market from 1902 to 1929; he scored exactly at chance with 45 right and 45 wrong.[35]

It is something of a wonder that consumers of financial forecasting continue to support a multi-billion dollar industry that can be simulated by flipping a coin. The evidence is over-whelming: financial markets are not logically predictable. Something extra—intuition—must be added to get an edge on chance.

Several comparison tests made by the *National Enquirer* between psychics and stock analysts have shown consistently better results for the psychics. The measuring rod was theoretical earnings or losses for stock or commodity picks. But the *National Enquirer* carries no weight in the financial Establishment.

'People would only accept psychic phenomena if there were a story on the front page of the *Wall Street Journal*,' predicted parapsychologist Russell Targ in August 1982. Targ, formerly at SRI International and now head of the National ESP Laboratory in Portola Valley, California, was reacting to skepticism about psychic phenomena expressed at the centenary meeting of the Society for Psychical Research in England.

Targ fulfilled his self-prophecy on 22 October 1984: *The Wall Street Journal's* front page announced: 'Did Psychic Powers Give Firm a Killing in the Silver Market?' The article describes the initial success of Delphi Associates, formed by Targ, psychologist Keith Harary and businessman Anthony White, in predicting silver futures:

Using the money put up by three investors, Delphi tried to forecast roughly how much silver prices would change between Thursday's closing and Monday's closing. In all of the first nine tries, Keith Harary made correct predictions. Delphi only got into the market on seven of them, but the investors still made 'in the middle six figures,' and Delphi got a commission [60,000 dollars commission on 120,000 dollars profit for investors].[36]

Note that Harary did not merely 'guess' the silver market changes nine times in a row. That would be the same left-brain guessing that has been proven so well not to work in financial prediction.

The technique used by Delphi is called 'associative remote viewing'. A researcher works out a code to associate certain objects with certain market changes. On Thursdays Harary looked into his own future on Mondays to feel and see what objects he was given by Targ. If, say, Targ handed him an apple, that would mean the market went up. A pencil might mean the market went down. Harary had no idea what the possible objects might be so he could avoid left-brain guessing and rely on right-brain pictures and other sense perceptions.

Delphi fell apart, though, when an investor pressed them for more and more predictions and wanted to cut their commission in half. A second series did not work, neither did a third series with another remote-viewer. Targ learned from these last unsuccessful tries that psychic functioning is adversely affected when greed becomes the chief motive.[37]

Organizing the National ESP laboratory, Targ set up an experimental silver-futures forecasting experiment with a hundred people from all walks of life. The experiment is not designed to make money. In fact, participants are urged not to invest. 'A playful attitude has long been associated with psychic success,' says Targ. People who are anxious about losing money—or too excited about winning it—become emotionally involved, and that interferes with psychic functioning. Using the same technique as before, but giving feedback by sending respondents photos of the targets, Targ analyzed the predictions for consensus. The initial predictions, reported in 1987, were right 25 times out of 36 attempts; The odds are 30 to 1 for this 69 per cent success level.

Readers interested in participating in this ongoing experiment can write National ESP Laboratory, 80 Hayfield Road, Portola Valley, CA 94025.

Targ's former colleague at SRI International, Harold Puthoff, found a way to use this same technique to make money for a charitable cause. The precognitive targets were daily outcomes in the commodities market for a particular commodity. Seven members of a school board (the charity) did 6 pilot trials and 30 market trials in which they invested 1–2,000 dollars. Their consensus predictions were right 21 times out of 30 attempts. Their 70 per cent accuracy rate gave them odds of 455 to 1, and a bottom-line profit of 25,000 dollars for their school.[38]

The evidence continues to mount that psychic functioning can be used successfully to foresee financial and commodity market changes. Yet the intuitive faculty is greatly influenced by people's motivation. As more groups attempt to turn their intuitive abilities into money-making ventures, they should soon find out under exactly what restrictions their abilities will function—and which conditions lead to failure.

Targ once calculated that a 75 per cent precognitive success rate, with 10,000 dollar investments at a time, would produce in a year of investing in silver futures the grand sum of a hundred trillion dollars. I believe that such a thing could never happen. Financial markets are a gamble. If they became a sure thing for one person, no one else would bet against him. So the markets would collapse. End of intuitive opportunity.

Economic Forecasting

Economists, whose predictions influence government and industry policies, have, like other computerized experts, not fared well in prophetic accuracy. The top 10 economic forecasting agencies' predictions for 1981 were analyzed in the *Los Angeles Times* by Robert Magnuson (3 January 1982):

> Even more than in past years, the economists were proved wrong by events in 1981. When they thought signs indicated that the economy would go into a slump, it rebounded. And when they said the economy was supposed to blossom, it wilted instead. Similarly, when the inflation rate was supposed to surge, it actually eased; then it surged when it was supposed to ease.
>
> But more embarrassing to the forecasters was the fact that they all failed to foretell the year's big economic events: the slide into the current deep recession, and the persistence of high interest rates.
>
> ... even some of their most vociferous critics acknowledge that the projections were thrown off in part by developments that caught everyone by *surprise*. [My italics.][39]

In early 1980 I had the opportunity to cross prophetic swords with four experts in economics in estimating the rate of inflation for the period beginning in 1982. The predictions were published in *The Book of Predictions* by David Wallechinsky, Amy Wallace and Irving Wallace (Morrow, 1981).[40] The experts predicted that inflation would be double digit and would accelerate. They were extrapolating from a database that showed inflation increasing. When we made our predictions, inflation was over 12 per cent. I predicted it would subside to 8 per cent by mid-1982.

In December 1981, top economic experts issued a revised short-term prediction for 1982 inflation: 8 per cent. They confirmed my more precise prediction made without benefit of analysis of economic data. My prediction was made in two steps. First, I assumed that the experts might be wrong. Second, I visualized a graph of the coming years' inflation rate and estimated the 1982 value as 8 per cent. I had no logical data to back up my prediction, but I did experience that 'gut feeling' that told me to pay attention to my mental picture.

Logic and Intuition

The trouble with scientific forecasting is that it assumes a surprise-free scenario of the future, whereas the future keeps hitting us with surprises. If only a few of those surprises can be foreseen by intuitive knowing, a dramatic increase of success in predicting will become possible.

In the first edition of this book I theorized: 'It's about time that forecasters began to use the right half of their brain to achieve a true science of prediction. When the two halves of the brain, logic and intuition, are combined, we are able to forecast on solid empirical data *and also* intuit some of those surprises.'

Supporting my theory is the work of David Loye, co-director of The Institute for Futures Forecasting in Carmel, California. He tested the predictive abilities of 135 students at three schools. Correlating their success at predicting political and economic events with their styles of brain functioning (left-brained, right-brained, or both), Loye found that students who were drawing upon both sides of the brain outscored both left and right-brained students. Loye interprets his findings for the science of prediction in this way:

These findings may indicate why, for example, forecasters of interest rates, market trends, and other economic matters are so often more wrong than right. Economists and others who are attracted to mathematics and the computer are generally *left-brain* dominant people who tend to suppress their right-brain capabilities. But these devalued right-brain inputs include the intuitive 'hunches' so meaningful to the successful entrepreneur, the detection of 'gestalts,' and the patterns within a bewildering array of data that can lead to the useful but *nonobvious* conclusion.

In this time of vast economic unsettlement, with fears of another Great Depression growing, it now seems obvious that the development of more 'balanced mind' approaches to economic forecasting is urgently needed.[41]

Loye's words ring as true today (even the fear of a Great Depression) as they did in 1982 when he wrote them. Yet his advice has not been heeded, which may explain why we have yet another round of fear of a Great Depression. Loye advocates training left-brain forecasters in right-brain activities such as art, music and meditation. I would also add psychic functioning, of course. He makes a sensible suggestion that forecasting be done by teams which counterbalance the left-brainers with the right-brainers and include more people with balanced brain functioning.

Training the Intuitive Mind

For over 50 years parapsychologists have been testing psychic abilities by asking people to guess which out of four or five target possibilities is the ESP target. The famous Zener or ESP cards used back in the 1930s at Duke University by J. B. Rhine's lab. were typical of this style of testing. Yet for most people, the more testing they did, the worse they got. This is because the old-fashioned testing methods actually extinguish psychic ability, leading to the infamous 'decline effect' in scores over time.

In the 1970s Russell Targ, then at SRI International, succeeded in getting NASA to spend 90,000 dollars on researching his ESP Teaching Machine. Subjects guessed which of four buttons was pre-programmed to light up next (clairvoyance). The device featured a pass button, which allowed subjects to skip some trials. Targ hoped that the subjects would be able to show ESP learning on this machine. (It later inspired a current hand-held device, the Perceptron.) Out of 147 subjects, 5 per cent showed either significant learning (with odds of 100 to 1) or high above-chance scoring. The overall results of the study came in at chance.

Importantly, though, not a single subject showed a significant decline. So Targ did improve on traditional testing methods by eliminating the decline effect. Yet his device did not work for 94 per cent of subjects.

Why was this? With four choices, for example, you will be wrong by chance 75 per cent of the time. There's nothing more boring than being 'just plain wrong'. Even worse, you will be right 25 per cent of the time just by chance—so you are getting 'false feedback', which confuses your subconscious mind. In this test people were just not getting the encouraging and sensitive kind of feedback that leads to development of intuitive skills.

Eight years of research into this problem led me to discover a new principle of psychic testing. I call the device I use to demonstrate this 'Psychic Reward: An Electronic Wheel of Fortune that Trains Intuition'. It was programmed by Jack Houck, an aerospace engineer, for IBM and Macintosh. The design, developed from roulette experiments, is an electronic wheel of fortune with a big difference: the closer you get to the Big Money (10,000 dollars), the higher you score in money points. Chance score is 1,000 dollars. A wheel with 26 segments, one for each letter of the alphabet, provides the target possibilities. You run your hand around the wheel to feel an impulse—a tingling or 'magnetic' pull—that might indicate where an arrow will randomly appear. When you press your guess letter, the program randomly chooses the arrow location. By giving rewards for getting close to the target, Psychic Reward enables trainees to develop their intuition with 96 per cent positive feedback. False feedback is reduced to less than 4 per cent. Your scores are automatically recorded and analyzed statistically. A chart shows your progress through 60 tests of 30 trials, a total of 1,800 trials, and a statistics screen gives the exact odds against chance. Researchers can determined how you got your score, and analyze for any inclines (suggestive of learning) in scoring. Counting also partial experiments, 44 per cent of subjects showed significant psi learning—seven lines better than Targ's ESP Teaching Machine.

Fifteen experiments have all shown the incline effect indicative of learning—against the enormous odds of 48,500 to 1.

The training teaches you to trust 'gut feelings' or other internal signals that accompany accurate predictions of random events. You learn how to recognize 'right-brain' messages that give you correct intuitive impressions. The real-life payoff comes when trainees develop their intuitive abilities to give them an edge on chance in predicting random events—in business and in life. A Canadian researcher, a medical doctor, used Psychic Reward to train himself to beat slot machines. He won 3,000 dollars in three days.

An earlier prototype, called 'Psychic Defender', which gives 50 per cent positive feedback, is available for Apple computers. It features a search beam to predict the precognition target in a wheel display. Advancement through four levels of 6, 10, 12, and 14 target segments comes as a reward for success. A chance score is 225 points. Designed as a competitive game, the program has no limit on how high you can score. The top 10 scores are displayed at the end of each game.

Expertise vs Intuition

Give two experts with the same background the same scientific data and ask them to predict the outcome, and you will get two different answers. One man's logic is another man's wild fantasy. The man with the greater scientific training is not necessarily the better prophet.

A friend who trained Orky, the 14,000-pound killer whale now at Sea World in San Diego, California, recently told me how intelligent his remarkable performer is. He described a feat he had taught Orky and asked me to estimate how long it took the animal to learn it. I said I had no idea. He urged me to guess. 'Four minutes,' I said.

'That's not fair,' my friend complained. 'You got the answer psychically. Any expert trainer would have said four to six weeks. It took Orky actually about three and a half minutes.'

Lacking any expertise in my friend's area of knowledge, I merely listened to whatever words popped into my head. But I honestly cannot say if what I said was psychic, intuitive, or just a good guess. The important thing was that my answer was right—or at least better than informed expertise might have given.

We all have the ability to come up with the right answer—if we are not seduced by the notion that logic takes precedence over intuition. How many times have you begun to answer some question off the top of your head correctly, only to find yourself saying, 'Oh, that can't be right because—[logical reason].' Intuitions are often vague, but they carry a conviction of rightness for those who have learned to listen to them. Someone who learns to balance logic and intuition to predict the future should be enormously successful—especially in making major business decisions.

Strong statistical support for this statement was gathered by two researchers at the Newark College of Engineering. When Douglas Dean and John Mihalasky gave precognition tests to company presidents, it was discovered that the successful presidents (those who had doubled their company profits in the last five years) scored above chance. Unsuccessful company presidents scored below chance. The precognition test—a computer card that would later have a hundred numbers chosen by random chance—was particularly well designed for businessmen since numbers are the bottom line in business. In their book, *Executive ESP*, Dean and Mihalasky offer fascinating stories of how financial wizards use their intuition to make bids that undercut the competition by a few hundred dollars when millions are at stake.[42] The right numerical answer can come only through intuitive, psychic processes. But the businessman has to be expert in logical understanding and manipulation of numbers as well. It is mostly at the top management level that decisions must be made for which insufficient data are available for logical analysis. Should we drill an oil well at location X? Should we merge with company B? Should we acquire company Y? Should we bid on contract C, and how much?

Questions like these are successfully answered by intuitive company presidents. The results of their decisions will not be known for a long time. What seems like a *logical* decision today may turn out to have a bad outcome tomorrow; what seems like an *illogical* decision today may have the best outcome in the future. All company presidents must demonstrate a high level of logical ability, but it is those who can also tap their intuitive, psychic abilities who will best foresee the 'surprises' that make the most lucrative business deals. A recent survey of over 2,000 managers by Weston Agor, head of the MBA program at the University of Texas, El Paso, discovered that across many industries the top managers scored higher in psychological questionnaires measuring intuitive capacities.[43]

A company president or financial wizard seldom brags about his or her intuition or ESP supplying the right answer. Rather, he or she manufactures a logical-sounding excuse for this foreknowledge. The financial community still regards ESP as kooky and distrusts the unknown. But when a chairman of the board retires, we hear the true stories of how he or she made millions for the company through hunches and intuition.

Shortly after he retired as chairman of the board of Phillips (66) Petroleum, William W. Keeler admitted that many of his successes came from paying attention to inner feelings. 'There were too many incidents that couldn't be explained merely as coincidences. I had successes in uncharted areas. My strong feelings toward things were accurate—when I would let myself go.'[44]

Pointing to his solar plexus, Keeler said, 'I get to feeling it right here, and it is very strong. In fact, it sometimes is so strong I think of it as fact.'

In one extraordinary example, Keeler told how he was able to project an engineering graph curve with only one data point. 'I saw an instantaneous value for pressure, temperature, and catalysis at one particular point, yet I can't tell you why or how I got it.'

My analysis for why: he needed the information. For how: his intuitive gut feeling worked its way up to his mind's eye to emerge as a full-scaled psychic impression with accurate details.

Keeler's experience typifies the balanced logical and intuitional brain functioning characteristic of scientific genius. Intent focus of attention on a problem combined with expert knowledge makes the sudden leap to the right answer in a flash of awareness that bypasses logical processes. *Eureka!* Afterward comes the studied application of logic to discover if the answer is indeed correct; the hows and whys must now be sought; testing must be done; ways to prove or disprove the instant insight require hard work of the logical mind.

Science textbooks present the path of discovery and knowledge as proceeding from diligent logic and sound thinking. But that's a cover-up. What really happens is that the answer comes first by creative, intuitional and psychic means, and the logical pathways to it are created later. One true case of scientific brilliance, however, is finally making it into the texts: Einstein discovered the principle of relativity at age 16 in an intuitive image in his mind's eye and then spent many years trying to prove it.

If our educational system tried to encourage creative and brilliant thinking, teachers would not reprimand Johnny for 'not paying attention' but would ask him, 'Johnny, what insights did you have just now while you were in your right-brain mode?'

Johnny's periods of 'not paying attention' happen about every 90 minutes, in the same rhythm as nocturnal dreams. Daydreams are closely linked to right-brain functioning, including intuition and ESP. In other words, daydreaming is conducive to future consciousness. Like nocturnal dreams, daydreams serve our primary needs from the unconscious but also scan our environment for future events that threaten or interest us. We can artificially induce dreams to provide pictures and words about the future. If we call our artificial dreams 'visions of the future', we are in the business of futurology.

Science-Fiction as Prediction

People who write their visions of the future in an entertaining, dramatic and vivid style are called science-fiction writers. People who document their scenarios of the future by research and who logically argue their visions are called scientific experts or futurists. Sometimes the two breeds are mixed, as in the person of Arthur C. Clarke, who writes both fiction and nonfiction predictions. In his 1958 study of the prophetic accuracy of both schools of prediction, *Profiles of the Future*, Clarke found that science-fiction writers, using their creative, intuitive approach, were far more accurate than their logical scientific brethren in forecasting dates of technological progress.[45] As it turned out, both schools of prediction overestimated the arrival times of future technologies. The marvels of tomorrow were here before anyone predicted they would be. The lesson should have been clear: intuition is superior to logic in prediction.

Clarke's own combination of logic and intuition has produced some excellent prophetic hits: In 1947 he predicted that the first rocket ship would land on the moon in 1959—a direct hit with the first Russian unmanned moon launch. He was only off by five months with his 1958 prediction of a manned moon landing in 1970 (Apollo 11 landed on 20 July 1969).

Arthur C. Clarke's famous dictum on whom to believe about the future states: 'When a distinguished but elderly scientist states that something is possible, he is almost certainly right. When he states that something is impossible, he is very probably wrong.'

Here is my dictum on science-fiction writers: 'When a distinguished science-fiction writer states personally that something is possible, he is almost always right. When his fiction says something is possible but he personally says it is impossible, his fiction should be given priority.'

As a good example of a science-fiction writer making a statement of personal belief that should be disregarded, here are the opening words of Arthur C. Clarke's nonfiction book *Profiles of the Future*: 'It is impossible to predict the future, and all attempts to do so in any detail appear ludicrous within a few years.'

As Exhibit One, I offer Clarke's 1953 masterpiece of science fiction, *Childhood's End*, which describes a future time in which children develop psychokinetic powers. In a disclaimer, Clarke disavowed any responsibility for this outrageous prediction: 'The opinions expressed in this book are not those of the author.'

In 1973, 20 years later, when Clarke was visiting London, he witnessed the Israeli psychic Uri Geller giving a psychokinetic demonstration. Geller's appearances on British television had galvanized thousands of children to copy his psychokinetic deeds—a few being accomplished under the watchful eyes of parapsychologists and physicists. According to an eyewitness friend at this demonstration, Geller appeared to dematerialize a part of a disc.

'My God!' exclaimed Clarke. 'It's all coming true. This is what I wrote about in *Childhood's End*. I can't believe it!'

Another science-fiction writer who shares Clarke's non-fictional disbelief in prediction is Robert Silverberg. In a 1980 interview he said, 'Science fiction does not predict—at least not in the usual sense. We look at patterns. We look for trends. We guess. It's hit and miss. When we aim for specific predictions, we miss enormously.'[46]

As Exhibit Two, I offer Robert Silverberg's 1975 novel, *The Stochastic Man*, which tells the story of a futurist scientist who develops his ability at precognition and combines the scientific and psychic aspects of prediction to achieve extraordinary accuracy. The stochastic man ('stochastic' means 'pertaining to guesswork') sets up a think tank to refine guesswork into clairvoyant prophecy.

When I read the book in 1975 I was working at a think tank in northern California as a subject in psychokinesis experiments. My co-subject in these experiments was a futurist scientist who had developed extraordinary abilities in various types of psychic functioning, including precognition. He told me how psychic methods were being combined with scientific methods to predict the future. I wrote Silverberg that his novel was in fact predicting the future of prediction, and that its beginnings were at hand.

The Future of Prediction

My real-life stochastic friend has asked to be anonymous, since, like the fictional stochastic man, he must conceal the source of his information lest it alarm his corporate and government clients.

Between bouts of disturbing a superconducting magnetometer, my stochastic friend told me how he and others at this think tank were synthesizing logic and ESP to come up with better answers. It turned out that many futurists were already using psychic techniques but did not realize it. They had not been tested for ESP—to them it was merely creative imagination about the future. But their techniques were nearly identical to those I use with students for psychic sensing of the future.

The method of combined logic and ESP (call it 'intuition' if it is vague) first requires a collection of scientific data about a problem or trend in society. Alternate scenarios about the future are developed from this data. Then intuitive future visioning is applied to project what will happen if these alternate scenarios come true. The futurist may project himself to the year 2000 and look backward to sense the most significant changes and how they might have arisen. He looks forward in his intuitive mode to sense the outcome of a particular scenario. Several people working on a project do this, and the consensus of their future projections is considered the best guess about the future. Usually there emerge not one but several possible futures—depending on society's choices.

The next stage in the future of prediction will be the development of 'surprise-sensing'. Since so many traditional futurist scenarios fail because they depend on being surprise-free, futurists' psychic talents will be trained to look for surprises by pure psychic methods. This new development will save governments and corporations billions of dollars that are now currently wasted on programs that fail because the future was not correctly anticipated.

The creation of a reliable 'consciousness technology' will be achieved as the art of prophecy merges with the science of prediction. If more and more people learn to tap their psychic potential to see into the future, and learn how to rely on this skill in their everyday life, society will soon feel the pressure to employ futurists and psychics (stochastic men and women) to envision possible futures and show which societal choices will lead to which futures.

Once precognition has emerged from the world of the strange into the everyday world of business, government, education and science, the stage will be set for a new leap forward: an enlightened society will have the wisdom to choose and fulfill its best future.

No matter how brilliant and talented psychics might become in predicting the marvels of the future, those marvels will not happen unless society acts to choose them.

Exercises

Looking Forward

1. Select some area of future development that interests you. It can be anything—technologies, entertainment, economics, for example. Review the subject and read what experts might predict. Probably you have read something recently that excites your interest and curiosity about the future.

2. Now relax and let all the logical information drain out of your mind. You might take a walk, or try meditation, chanting, singing in the shower, or just listening to music. Close your eyes and focus your attention *out there*—as if time were palpably in front of you.

3. Shift your awareness to the future, visualizing it in your mind's eye as a series of waves in the ocean of time. Now introduce your target. Let the target float across the time waves until it stops. Estimate how far away in years it might be.

4. Now ask specific questions about your target. What advantages might come from this future development? How might it change people's way of life? How might it change your life?

5. In evaluating your answers, give more credence to those images that appeared in visual form and that seemed to be accompanied by a strong gut feeling or activation of the solar plexus.

6. If no specific year came, try reciting the dates of the years ahead and pay attention to your gut feeling for giving you the right answer.

7. If you know other people who share your interest in this future development, ask them to do the same experiment. But don't tell them beforehand what you saw.

8. Collect their predictions and examine them for any sort of consensus.

9. If your prediction and any consensus group prediction goes against what the experts think, register your prediction with American Prophecy Project, 357 Bowery, New York, NY 1003.

10.

The Flexible Future

Can we change the future? When psychics prevision a future event that does not come to pass, is it because they are wrong? Or because they foresaw a possible future that was changed? When disaster is foreseen, can that disaster be prevented? Let's look at the evidence.

Foreordained Fate

In the annals of psychical research there are a number of stories of people who had a premonition of some disaster or death but were unable to prevent it. Such a premonition came to Robert Morris, Sr, an American agent for a Liverpool shipping firm in the eighteenth century. His son, Robert Morris, Jr, a framer of the American Constitution, tells the story in his biography of his father. The night before the elder Morris was to meet the ship *Liverpool* at a port in Maryland, he dreamed that he received a mortal wound from a cannon salvo fired in his honor. Morris told the ship captain of his premonition and said he thought it would be best to skip that landing party. The captain dismissed his dream as superstition and convinced Morris to attend. Morris obtained the captain's promise that the salute would not be fired until he or the captain gave the signal. So the captain told the gunner not to fire until he raised his hand.

Morris and the captain went to meet the ship in a rowboat. A fly alighted on the captain's nose, causing him to raise his hand to brush it away. The gunner thought it was the signal and fired the cannons—directly into Morris. Wadding embedded itself in Morris's arm, causing an infection that led to his death a few days later. Robert Morris's foreknowledge of his death was insufficient to prevent it. But note that it was his own choice to be talked into attending the landing party. His fate was self-ordained.

Preventing Disaster

In February 1981, a San Jose area woman, Mrs Frances Vernier, awoke with a horrifying dream that one of the nursing homes she ran was going up in flames—helpless old people were being burned to death in their beds. The dream premonition woke Mrs Vernier at two in the morning; she sat in her rocking chair until dawn worrying. Unable to bear it any longer, she drove to the Saratoga Place Convalescent Center in the early morning to check out the house. She was about to leave when she discovered a fire burning around gas pipes near the furnace in the rear of the building. She told a nurse to call the fire department and got the residents out of the house.[47]

When I read of this account I telephoned San Jose County Fire Chief Victor Marino, who testified that it was true. 'With her dream and her intuition, Mrs Vernier prevented a major disaster. In just a few more minutes there would have been an explosion—and these people would have been killed,' Chief Marino said. He added, 'I never believed in ESP, but this proves there's something to it.' It also proves that it is possible to avert a tragedy by acting on foreknowledge of a possible future.

I, too, have such a story. In February 1975 I gave a lecture on premonitions to a class at St Mary's College in the East Bay of San Francisco. The next day the class teacher, a friend, telephoned to warn me that one of the students had a premonition that I might be involved in an accident on 19 April. She relayed the student's warning that I should avoid traveling on that date.

Well, as things turned out, I did find myself traveling that weekend. My wife drove me to Monterey to give a lecture. I told her about the premonition, and she was keeping an extra watchful eye on traffic. After the lecture, about two in the morning of 19 April, as we were returning to our hotel after stopping at a nightclub, I said, for no particular reason, 'Let's make a left hand turn here.'

Diane stopped to make the turn, even though we had a green light. At that instant a car speeded through the intersection—through a red light—at about 50 miles an hour. I breathed a sigh of relief and said, 'That was our accident. We don't have to worry anymore.' And so we spent the rest of 19 April without cause for alarm.

Apparently my inner self scanned the environment for the

speeding car and gave me the impulse to suggest a turn.

Predicted events that *almost happen but do not* constitute the strongest evidence we have that the future is flexible, that it responds to human consciousness and choice. The flexible future necessarily limits the accuracy of precognition.

This theoretical argument came to a practical case in point on Easter Sunday in 1972, when I gave a lecture to science-fiction writers and fans at the New York City Lunacon. I described a premonition that a canister aboard the next flight to the moon, Apollo 16, would explode and cause the death of an astronaut. After the talk, a famous science-fiction writer approached me and made a remark that seemed to contradict his public skepticism about precognition: 'You know, perhaps it would be worth the death of one astronaut to convince people of the reality of these things.'

'I thought of that, too,' I replied, reflecting that I had just told the group that I would make no more predictions of disaster unless something could be done to prevent it. I wrote Edgar Mitchell, a backup astronaut for Apollo 16, and detailed to him my premonition. I ended my letter with the words 'Let us pray.'

Apollo 16 went to the moon and back without mishap. But when a canister was taken back to the factory for examination, it exploded. Many people were injured. If the canister had exploded aboard the moon flight, it might well have killed an astronaut.

Was I foreseeing a possible disaster that was somehow averted? The question came into sharper focus in 1981, as preparations were being made for the space shuttle *Columbia*'s maiden test flight and landing.

Previsions of *Columbia*

As the much-postponed space-shuttle *Columbia* was being readied for its first flight, a television documentary showed the problems that had put it two years behind schedule. The most persistent problem was the more than 30,000 heat-shield tiles that had to be bonded one by one on the craft. If just one of them fell off the underside, the searing heat of re-entry into the atmosphere—reaching 2,800 degrees—could lead to a disastrous fire.

After watching the documentary I did a psychic reading on the future of the shuttle, and sent my 6 January prediction to NASA engineer Fred Kolb and the Central Premonitions Registry. (All the predictions quoted in this section were also registered with the

CPR.) I foresaw a beautiful takeoff on 12 April, though it was scheduled for 17 March. On re-entry I foresaw a tile falling off the rear of the craft, leading to a rough landing and injury to the pilot on the left (John Young).

On 22 January I dreamed of the craft coming in too fast, swinging around and breaking the right wing.

On 13 March I had the opportunity to ask psychic Beverly Jaegers about her impressions of the shuttle when we met in Atlanta on the child-killer case. Holding photos of the *Columbia*, she felt that something might fall off the rear of the craft. She foresaw a rough landing in which the right wing would break off. She was not certain her impressions applied to the first flight. But I was struck by the similarity in our impressions. Jaegers mentioned at the time her almost exact impressions might be coincident to being handed the material by me.

I convinced the Mobius Society that a psychic probe should be done on the *Columbia* with their team of psychics spread across the country and in Italy and Canada. Five respondents, including Jaegers and myself, foresaw danger. Another respondent described a computer malfunction very similar to the one that delayed the launch from 10 April to 12 April. The Central Premonitions Registry received 10 premonitions of disaster for the *Columbia*.

I was frantically worried about the *Columbia* and wrote Cable News Network in Atlanta on 4 April in the hope that I might be able to appear on the program *Freeman Reports* to alert NASA to present dangers so that they could postpone the 10 April launch to correct the defects. I knew from my experience with Apollo 16 that NASA's reaction to premonitions is to cross fingers.

At five in the afternoon on 7 April I received a strong impression that the space shuttle was saved. Somehow, in some mysterious way, our psychic data seemed to be acted upon. Now I foresaw the *Columbia* coming in for a beautiful landing. I wrote Cable News to cancel my request for an appearance. I felt jubilant that the space shuttle would work and inaugurate a new age of technology. I even conceived the notion that I would like a ride in it.

On 9 April at 1.09 p.m., I received the impression that the 10 April launch would be postponed. I notified *The New York Times*. A computer malfunction postponed the launch until 12 April.

On takeoff some tiles fell from the rear of the craft. NASA engineers were so certain that tiles would *not* fall off that they had canceled an order for two tile-repair kits. Astronauts Young and Crippen brought the craft in for a beautiful landing, watched by millions on television.

I was so elated when the *Columbia* landed that I began to sing a song to my small children, 'I Want to Make My Dreams Come True'. My repeated visualizations of the *Columbia* coming in for a perfect landing, my dream, had come true. I bought the kids ice cream to celebrate.

Later I received a letter from Beverly Jaegers, written just before the landing, in which she told me that her final impression early in the morning of 8 April was that the craft would make a beautiful landing.

Somehow the crash landing we both had seen a month before was averted, and we both knew it as the time came near. Jaegers wondered if perhaps her impression on 13 March had come telepathically from me. That certainly is a possibility—indeed, one that I worried about at the time. But in view of the 13 other premonitions of disaster, I tend to think we both were picking up the same possible future that was averted.

The big question is how? Perhaps there were millions of other people who also visualized and strongly hoped for a beautiful landing. Perhaps our collective consciousness changed the future. Somehow it was changed by 5.00 p.m. PDT on 7 April 1981.

The *Challenger* Disaster

The space shuttle program operated so smoothly for five years that the public lost interest in watching launches—until the *Challenger* was launched on 28 January 1986. After 73 seconds, the spacecraft exploded into wildly veering smoke trails. 'A major malfunction,' announced an incredulous NASA voice.

The 1982 edition of this book predicted that a 'shuttle launch will have severe malfunctions that could threaten the space program.'

A 1981 report submitted to NASA engineer Fred Kolb in Virginia contained an interview I had done with Beverly Jaegers about the upcoming launch of *Columbia*. She began by saying that her comments might apply to another shuttle carft:

> I'm getting an impression of something structurally insecure toward the rear end of the craft. Something possibly could be a victim of thrust ... Something could be loosened ... during the thrust propulsion of this vehicle. But it seems to be a sort of wrap-around ring ... connected to the propulsion system itself. There's also the possibility of leakage before anything more dramatic would occur.

There is a problem with one of the components of the propulsion system, right at the rear of the tail plane assembly, and it is not seated properly. It could possibly cause a leak and, possibly because of thrust, disengage.

Kolb now made additional annotations on Jaeger's prediction:

Her impressions were most exact and most accurate as far as they went. Her comment or impressions of 'leaking before anything more dramatic would occur' was exactly on target. The impressions of improper seating (of the O-ring) has proven to be correct.

The presidential panel investigating the *Challenger* disaster showed that an O-ring (a wrap-around ring) toward the rear of the right booster rocket (part of the propulsion system) had leaked gases and triggered the explosion. Jaegers has succinctly described in layman's terms exactly what the problem was. But, as so often happens, she was uncertain of the time. Yet, as Kolb pointed out, *all* shuttles had the potential for the same malfunction.

I believe, in this case, that the fatal flaw of the shuttle design could no longer be evaded. The flexible future had reached its limit.

Project Chicken Little

The earthward plunge of *Skylab* in 1979 provided my first opportunity for investigating the flexible future—and a chance to cross prophetic swords with NASA. Using the most sophisticated electronic and computer methods in the world, NASA was attempting to predict when *Skylab* would fall to earth. As to precisely *where* it would fall, a NASA scientist spokesman assessed their computer prediction capability with the statement: 'There's no way in hell you can predict where it's going to fall.'

To William Braud, a parapsychologist at Mind Science Foundation in San Antonio, Texas, the coming demise of *Skylab* at an unknown place and time provided an opportunity for a mass precognition test, which he called Project Chicken Little.[48] I was one of 512 people who sent in their predictions of 'the currently unknown impact location and impact time of *Skylab*'. To get the location I psychically dowsed a small map Braud had sent to get a longitude and latitude; where the two lines met indicated my predicted target location: off the west coast of Africa, just above the equator. I also sent in a time prediction but later revised it because of a reaction that my wife and I had to NASA's prediction of 'Chicken Little Day'.

On 30 May 1979, when Diane and I were reading *Newsweek's* report on Chicken Little Day, she objected that a better metaphor would be 'Icarus Day', since the sun was driving *Skylab* down four years too soon—much as it had melted Icarus's wings and plunged him into the sea. Our discussion of Icarus led us to a 1969 book of poetry in which the fall of Icarus was described on page 437, line 16. A strange, emotionally heightened feeling made us wonder if the book contained a code prophetic of *Skylab's* fall.

North American Air Defense Command (NORAD), with its 20-station tracking network, predicted that *Skylab* would start its final descent between 20 June and 14 July, with Chicken Little Day being 2 July. Yet our book of poetry, page 437, line 16, suggested 16 July with the possible hour as 4.30 p.m., and, as I guessed later, 4.37. I sent my revised prediction time to Project Chicken Little and waited to see if NASA and NORAD would revise their predictions.

A week later, on 7 June NORAD joined our book of poetry to predict 16 July. An unexpected lull in radiation bursts from the sun was keeping *Skylab* up for two more weeks. On 21 June, NASA radioed *Skylab* to turn sideways to increase atmospheric drag and, they hoped, avoid population centers. This changed NORAD's prediction for Chicken Little Day to 12 July.

Also on 21 June I gave a press conference in San Francisco. The two major San Francisco papers, the Oakland paper, two television stations and several radio stations carried my prediction: Chicken Little Day was to be 16 July, with the two largest pieces of *Skylab* to land at 4.30 and 4.37 p.m. local Africa time off the west coast of Africa.

NASA and NORAD changed Chicken Little Day to 11 July, but still did not know where and precisely when *Skylab* would come down.

On 11 July, precisely at 4.37 p.m. local time off the west coast of Africa, *Skylab* lost radio contact as it broke up into pieces. It rained space junk over a 4,000-mile track across Australia. As soon as the breakup time was radioed across the nation, I received a telephone call from fellow precognition researcher Fred Blau, who had also entered the Chicken Little Day sweepstakes.

'My God!' exclaimed Fred. 'You got the exact *minute*!' Blau had converted Pacific Daylight Time to local time off the west coast of Africa to realize the significant correspondence with my prediction of 4.37 p.m. The media, of course, did not, and anyway it was the wrong day. But for the record, the odds of guessing the minute and time zone of the breakup would be 34,560 to 1.

What does this tell us about the flexible future? NASA's decision on 21 June to turn *Skylab* changed Chicken Little Day from our mutual prediction of 16 July to 11 July. NASA changed the future. Yet my 4.37 p.m. correspondence suggests there was a predetermined aspect to Chicken Little Day as well. Computers are unable to predict the outcome of such theoretically random events; human beings do better.

On the final scorecard of Project Chicken Little, not a single person of the 512 guessed correctly the impact location and time. But those predictions were registered before NASA started fooling around with *Skylab*. It seems to me quite likely that if the predictions had been gathered *after* 21 June there would have been a consensus prediction close to the Chicken Little Day time and place.

Personal Choices

Our lives are full of choices. Sometimes we never know what could have happened if we had made a different choice. Sometimes we feel sure we made the right choice; at other times we feel just as sure we made the wrong choice. Just how much personal choice does the flexible future allow us?

Here is a parable of choice.

In 1972, while living in New York, I gave psychic readings for two friends, one an off-off Broadway actor and his friend, an off-off Broadway playwright. I told the actor that I saw a great future ahead of him as a star in Western movies. For the playwright I predicted a hit Broadway play.

Three months later the actor received a telegram from Western movie director Sam Peckinpah asking him to do a screen test for the lead of Peckinpah's next film, *Pat Garrett and Billy the Kid*. The actor panicked; he was, his friends said, fearful of success, or fearful of failing. He chose not to make the screen test. He did not fulfill the prediction. Kris Kristofferson played Billy the Kid.

Two years later, now living in San Francisco, I had the opportunity of seeing my prediction for the playwright brought to life on the stage. Robert Patrick's *Kennedy's Children* was such a hit on Broadway that it was taken on a national tour. I could boast that Patrick had fulfilled my prediction. But it is Patrick who gets the credit, not me. He recognized my prediction as one of his own guiding images and did his best to fulfill it. It was his choice and his creativity that led to fulfillment of his inner destiny.

Free Will versus Destiny

If we have an inner destiny—blueprint of life—how can we exercise our free will to make choices? For centuries the debate about free will versus destiny has misconstrued the whole matter of choice. We do not follow a destiny enforced upon us by some outside divinity; we are not puppets on a string. We follow an inner destiny *of our own choice*. Yes, we have blueprints—both biological and psychic—that limit us with our inborn potentials. But in the most important arena of choice—moral choice—our free will is supreme.

Many people speak of cause and effect. I prefer to speak of choice and consequence. Our inner destinies, like the rest of the universe, contain the seeds of the flexible future. When we choose which seed of our inner destiny to nourish, we plant the future consequences of our lives. Our lives do not just happen. They are created by our choices and the harvest we reap is our consequence.

We may choose to create challenges for ourselves so that we can learn. We may choose *against* the best blueprint of our inner self; the consequences will be disharmony and dissatisfaction with life. But sometimes, it is the worst of times that teach us the most—if we realize that it was our choice that gave us our present consquences. If we blame the universe or God or persons X, Y, and Z, we have not learned a thing—and probably will have to repeat the lesson.

Once we understand that it is we who are the masters of our universe—who make the choices that create the consequences of our lives—we become attuned to the very best that we can do and begin to fulfill our inner destiny. We influence the flexible future to go our way.

Often we make choices without much consideration of the future consequences. But if we learn to foresee the consequences of our choice, we learn to make better choices—how to foresee and fulfill our future.

Looking Backward

From the vantage point of tomorrow, you can more clearly see the consequences of a present choice. The 'Looking Backward' technique, also used by futurists, has several advantages over visiting psychics and counselors: it doesn't cost anything, it supplies the best answers (because they are yours), and you are more likely to act on your answers than on a stranger's advice.

When you are faced with a major choice in life, it is time to project yourself into the future and look back. A way to gain confidence in your ability to do this is to try it out with minor choices that give you feedback relatively soon: Will I like this movie? Will the boss like my new idea? Will my guests like a new recipe for dinner? What will happen if I decide to make a trip to Z?

To answer those questions, project your mind into the future just afterward and look back at the results. By paying attention to your feelings, you will quickly acquire the knack of intuitively choosing to do the right thing—both for yourself and others.

A related technique, which we shall explore in the Exercise section, is 'Attending Your Own Funeral'. By journeying through time to attend your own funeral and listening to what people are saying about you, you may find out what is really important to you while you can still act on it.

These techniques fail when you try to project some strongly held fantasy from your ego self. In analyzing the imagery, you should review the criteria for sifting true images from false.

Bear in mind that our conscious minds—to maintain our sanity—must shut out details of events that we cannot now act upon. A strong assurance from our inner self that things will work out in the future because we have seen them, does not mean that we can now relax and let the future happen by itself.

The greatest lesson that the flexible future can teach us is that the future is created now. Our present choices and decisions select which possible future will become our reality. The future is created by our minds.

Exercises

Looking Backward

1. Think of a major choice in your life just now. What are the options? List two possibilities that appeal to you.
2. Let your mind travel five years into the future. In your mind's eye, look back over the intervening years and ask how things worked out with the first choice. Did it fulfill your expectations? Pay attention to your gut feeling about the final outcome. How was your life changed by your choice?
3. Repeat the same questions with the second choice.
4. Now compare your feelings and reactions to the outcomes of

the two choices. Did one of them give a clearer picture and a better feeling? Did one of them seem dim and give you an anxious feeling?

5. Write down the choice that gave you the best feeling and seemed clearest. Now review it against the criteria of sifting false images from true in Chapter 6.

6. If your choice passed the test, consider how you might best be able to act on it.

7. If neither choice seemed really right, try projecting yourself once again into the future and ask, 'How did I resolve the situation? What did I finally decide to do?'

8. Did you discover in your attempts at looking backward something that surprised you? You may have found a guiding image that you didn't know you had.

Attending Your Own Funeral

1. Let your consciousness travel to the distant future for your funeral. You do not know what year it is or what the cause of death is; you know merely that people are gathering together to talk about you and your contributions. Friends and relatives are asking questions about you and making comments about how they judged your life.

2. In your mind's eye and ear eavesdrop on a conversation about you. You must be objective in your reaction to what they say. Your consciousness must merely record what is said so that you can react to it later.

3. Are they talking about what you accomplished in life? What were your most outstanding achievements?

4. Are they talking about the things you should have done but didn't? What was left undone?

5. Are they talking about how you helped and influenced others? How did your life enrich the lives of others?

6. Are they talking about your family? Did they have much to be grateful for? Were there things you should have done for them but didn't?

7. Now make notes of what you saw and heard. List them in two columns: a) Satisfying; b) Things to Be Done. Look over your list of things to be done and consider ways of doing them now.

8. Were there any surprises in the comments people made about you? If so, they might be guiding images that will assume importance in the future.

9. Did any of the comments made at your funeral suggest some action or choice that is pending right now? If so, did the experience give you any inspiration for present deeds?

11.

Shaping your Future

How can we make our positive prophecies of life self-fulfilling? How do we make our dreams come true? Once we have found our dreams—our true guiding images of life—we must find the ways that work best to bring them into reality.

We are brought up to believe that honest toil, sweat of the brow, determined faith in oneself, courage and perseverance will achieve our dreams. Those are all good ways, but the most important thing is lacking in that prescription for shaping our future: the mind. It is the mind that creates our dreams and the mind that shapes our future. If we master the understanding of the ways the mind works best, we begin to master the ways in which our dreams come true.

Scientific Research

Most people don't realize that the subject of parapsychology is really the study of how the mind creates reality. The scientific research done by parapsychologists in investigating the creative powers of the mind is hardly known outside of a small group of people interested in psychic phenomena. Technical terminology creates a barrier to understanding for the average person, but the fundamental findings of psychic research apply to the daily activities of every living soul. These findings can teach us how to use our minds to influence and shape our present and future. They can teach us how to overcome disease, how to achieve goals, how to accomplish miracles.

Perhaps you already follow some teaching that promises this sort of understanding. There must be hundreds of philosophies and religions that all claim to have the answers to such questions of basic lifemanship. These different approaches to understanding have one thing in common: they are untested; we must take them on faith. It is the business of science to test claims and differing approaches. By repeated experiment the truth comes to light. In that way we can free ourselves from centuries of accumulated error through the transmission of philosophical and religious teachings.

The first question that parapsychology asked about the creative power of the mind was: Can the mind influence external reality? Calling this mind power *psychokinesis* and defining it as 'the direct influence of mind on matter without any known intermediate physical energy', parapsychologists established that we can use our minds to change random events that are electronically generated by machines. Sixteen such experiments done between 1970 and 1975 yielded odds against chance of 10,000,000,000 to 1.

Psychokinesis (or PK for short) has been so well proven to exist that now the main research efforts have shifted to finding out how to make it work better. What mental strategies work best in which situations? There was already an enormous popular literature that purported to give the answers. But, until the mid-1970s, no one ever thought to test them.

At the University of California at Santa Barbara, parapsychologist Dr Robert Morris gave his students an assignment with far-reaching consequences. He asked them to read and digest as many books as they could find that purported to tell how best to use psychic powers. The class found 74 books by 57 authors, mostly at the airport news-stands—hence the project's name: The Airport Project. The students found that two basic methods were advocated for shaping the future:

1. Process imaging—imagining in the mind's eye the details of the process leading up to the desired goal.
2. Goal imaging—imagining the goal in its final fulfillment without concern for how it happens.

The next undertaking of the Santa Barbara research team was to find out which technique worked better. Using college students and others of the same age, Morris and his colleagues did two studies to investigate the difference in these techniques when the students were trying to influence random event generators and getting feedback on their success. The *process* technique gave only chance results. And worse, the students who had no prior experience in mind training got below-chance results with process imagery. They were trying to imagine just how the machine might be affected by their thought but found that the machine did the opposite of what they wanted.

The *goal* technique, however, worked beautifully. The students racked up odds against chance of 10,000 to 1 when they imagined that they would get the desired result without worrying just how the machine worked. They foresaw the future in its final form—and it happened.[49]

A similar study undertaken at Yale University by Ariel Levi with 51 psychology students as subjects showed that the goal technique worked best when feedback was given. When the students didn't know how they were doing, the process technique worked better.[50]

Not only did the Santa Barbara and Yale studies show the best ways to influence the future, they also showed that average college students are able to use their minds to affect external reality. PK, it now seems, is something that nearly anyone can do. Perhaps even every person can do it—or so I theorize—if the situation and the motivation are right.

I have years of experience in working with machines to demonstrate PK, and I can testify that it is far easier to work with human beings. The easiest situation in which to exert mind force is in affecting your own body. The greatest motivation comes when you are seriously ill, when medical science has given you up, and the only way to recover or prolong your life is to use your mind force to overcome physical disease.

Terminal cancer is the most dreaded disease we can have. 'Terminal' means that doctors have already scheduled you for demise; medical treatment can neither prevent death nor, in many cases, even prolong life. It is such conditions that give rise to extraordinary motivations—for some. Others take their medical prophecy of doom to heart and fulfill it on schedule.

Those who want to fight with all their powers can find a champion in Carl Simonton, M.D., at his clinic in Pacific Palisades, California.

Simonton advocates the use of mental power—process imaging—to accompany traditional cancer therapies. A stay at his clinic is expensive, but many highly motivated 'incurable' cancer patients have stayed there to try to lick the big C.

Simonton asks his patients to visualize their immune system as being very strong and destroying their cancer cells, which are to be seen as weak and disorganized. The patients choose their own visualizations—often like cartoon creatures seen on TV commercials. The good cells in white devour the bad cells in black.

The process style of imagery is used because the feedback to the patients takes a long time. But it does work. Of 240 terminal patients treated between 1973 and 1980, the median survival rate is twice as high as those treated with conventional therapies only. And the really good news is that 10 per cent of patients have dramatic remission of their cancers.[51]

Perhaps the greatest wonder of this work is that it is not available at *every* cancer clinic. The techniques are simple, the results a clear-cut improvement on traditional therapies, and there should be no lack of patients who would like to try to beat that death sentence. But apparently medical politics take precedence over the Hippocratic oath. As it seems to me, clinics will offer mind techniques only when patients demand it as their right in the pursuit of health.

Simonton's former wife and colleague, Stephanie, is currently pursuing more rigorous scientific research in comparing conventional and mind–treatment therapies. Even now the growing popularity of meditation is achieving results that mystify the medical profession. On ABC's *Nightline* topic 'Mind Over Body' (21 December 1987), reporter Gail Harris said, 'A large insurance company compared 2,000 people who meditated with 600,000 who did not. The company found the meditators had 44 per cent fewer visits to the doctor, 55 per cent fewer tumours, and 87 per cent fewer cases of heart disease.' While the medical community continues to seek explanations, the miracle stories multiply.

An even greater success at treating cancer and other diseases with mind power will come when biofeedback techniques are utilized so that the goal strategy can be used. Patients will visualize themselves returning to perfect health, as being already well, and will receive signals from machines that measure their moment-to-moment progress. The greater effectiveness of goal strategy with feedback should dramatically increase the number of those who have remissions from terminal conditions.

Learning to Use your Mind

Our minds are used not only as computers for storing and retrieving information but also as creative tools for shaping our reality. It takes practice to get the mind working at its most effective level to realize our goals. It also takes feedback so that we know when we are doing something right. That is why the machines used in parapsychology are so useful: they are marvelous devices for training the mind to work little miracles.

Over the years I have had the opportunity of working with many types of PK-measuring machines and devices, usually in laboratory experiments. In every case, I received feedback—the secret for strengthening mind power. I learned litle by little just which strategy worked best with which machine. The more I learned, the easier it became. Part of that learning may, in fact, be merely the building of belief that one can do it. Once you have seen that your mind can affect a laser beam or a magnetometer or a random number generator, you believe it. It gives you confidence for the next impossible task.

Feedback is essential for the initial stages of learning, but once you have the hang of it, you can proceed without continual feedback. You can go ahead and create that future reality in the calm confidence that you know what you are doing. You *expect* your goal will be achieved because you have visualized it—you have seen it happen—and you know from experience that you are right.

So my translation of the Santa Barbara and Yale studies for use in everyday life is that feedback is needed for everyday initial success of goal oriented imagery. But one you have learned that seeing is believing—that seeing your goal accomplished in your mind's eye is believing that it will happen—you have mastered the simple but effective technique of shaping your future.

I add a gimmick to that technique. It has not been tested in the laboratory but I find it works like a charm; so do my students. When I visualize the results of my goal, I see enthusiastic applause and cheering. Sometimes I even see that redoubtable character from the Muppets, Kermit the Frog, applauding with his unrestrained and heart-felt enthusiasm because I did so well. And who could doubt the sincerity of Kermit the Frog?

When I see and enjoy this tremendous applause and cheering in my mind's eye for something I have accomplished in the future, I ask myself: 'What on earth did I do to provoke all that? It must be good. So I guess I should let myself do whatever it is that gets that kind of response.'

When my future goal is applause, I find it helps me to get out of the way of my bumbling self, which worries a lot. I just assume that I'll get the inspiration when I need it; that I shall do the right thing at the right time; that others will respond in kind and that we'll all have a good time.

I have come to realize what should have been obvious to anyone. We exert the greatest PK effect on ourselves. When we project an outcome in our minds—when we see a goal fulfilled—we influence ourselves to fulfill it. And when we act to make the visualized goal a reality, we do indeed affect the external universe.

And there's an added benefit. Once we begin to use our creative mind force to make our dreams come true—to fulfill our inner destiny—the rest of the universe finds our dream irresistible. Others co-operate and help. They find in our dream a part of their own dream. We work with them and they work with us to make our dreams a reality.

The inanimate universe is also responsive to our mind powers. So-called 'things' behave as if they have a consciousness; that consciousness wants to help, too.

We can become masters of our universe—not *the* universe, but *our* universe—in the same way that we are masters of our dream worlds, our bodies, our perceptions, our beliefs, our experience. The only universe we *can* know is our universe. So why shouldn't we be masters of all that we perceive and know?

The best way that we can learn to use our minds is to create an ideal universe that others will enjoy sharing. Our universe penetrates all the universes of all the people whose lives we touch. We share a dream. We share the ways in which we make our dreams come true. Our guiding images dovetail with their guiding images. Together we use our mind powers to shape a future that belongs to us all.

The Path of Fulfillment

Religions often teach that the path of fulfillment is achieved by following the example of the religion's founder. Christians say, 'Follow the example of Christ.' But somehow Christ's message that everyone has the capability to do what he did is ignored. The following things he did should have set the example for being a good Christian: prophesy, heal the sick, materialize food for the hungry, advise fishermen where fish may be found (clairvoyance), identify those who would betray him (telepathy), forgive those who did betray him (love), and materialize in a bodily form after death to show that he is eternal.

Christ said that it was 'the Father within' who did the work, that each of us has a spark of divinity that accomplishes miracles, that belief would enable us to emulate him.

But strangely, modern Christians make little attempt to emulate the wonders of Christ. Some groups of Christians even teach that the wondrous miracles of 'the Father within' are the work of the devil! Others who call themselves Christians even deny that we possess the abilities to 'do the work'. A strange condition indeed for a religion that is founded on what I might call 'psychic potential'. In the early days of Christianity every good Christian was expected to learn how to do psychic readings ('prophesying'), healing the sick, and channeling the Holy Spirit for 'speaking in tongues'.

Some Eastern religions teach that psychic phenomena get in the way of the path of fulfillment—that fulfillment comes only in a mystical union with God. In those traditions psychic abilities are mainly abused as sideshow attractions to impress the credulous with the godhood of the performer. It did not occur to ancient religious philosophers in those traditions that psychic abilities can be used to make a heaven, or Nirvana, on earth; they believed that Nirvana can be found only beyond the physical. So they paid scant attention to the now because the next existence beyond death is the only one with meaning. That slant can lead, and has led, to a great deal of present misery.

Attempting to strip away a few thousand years of misunderstanding, I find the core of most religious thought to be this. We are created in the image of God. We have a divinity, or creative consciousness, that partakes of the universe, that it is holographic and creates its own universe by means of its powers of mind. Created in the image of God, we are not only endowed with His powers but also His destiny: to create our own universes, to discover our inner destiny and fulfill it by prophesying and creating our future.

We do this not by listening to sermons or reading books but by discovering that it is we who have the keys to the kingdom, we who can unlock the mysteries of the mind to reveal our individual paths of fulfillment. Right here and now.

The fulfillment of our individual destinies does not happen as a solitary act. It can happen only in the context of human society. For society also has a destiny, and when we partake of that collective destiny we fulfill not only our own goals but those of the larger community. We help each other achieve a collective dream. True guiding images from our inner self stress the development of loving capabilities, healing and helping potentials, teaching and nurturing roles for the benefit of our young. The future of our dreams and the destiny of our collective civilization lie in the hands of our children. Thus our primary goal for self-fulfillment becomes the teaching of our children how best to fulfill their own lives.

We are poised on the brink of the next brave step in human evolution—a step that will take us closer to the day when every human being born into this world will have the opportunity to create his ideal universe. We adults are occasionally reminded that we use only a small portion of our mind and brain powers, but the scientists who tell us this never tell us how to increase our abilities, how to use that extraordinary reserve of mind force. We must learn for ourselves. One thing we should know for sure: if one person can do it, so can the rest of us. Once we see that the goal is possible, we can become like Olympic champions who set new records each year in perfecting the performance of the human instrument.

We who know of our potential path to a new evolutionary stage will act to fulfill it. Yet there will be many who prefer to complain that they don't know how, who think that young people should fend for themselves, who are satisfied with an absence of pain as their highest goal in life, and who are skeptical that the human condition can improve.

My advice to us who know better is to go ahead and do the best we can. Don't try to convert the skeptics; they will have to find out for themselves. If we set a few examples, if we show, through the abundant living of our lives, that we are indeed progressing toward this next step, it might occur to the others that they are missing out on something. They might just begin to get curious enough to suspend their disbelief. And once they open their minds, they might begin to join us. Our hope lies not in argument but in deeds.

Synchronizing with the Universe

How do we know if we are truly following our inner destiny—truly realizing our guiding images? We may be visualizing some wonderful goal in the far future. How do we know if we are on the right track?

There is only one way to know for sure. When feedback from the universe is positive—if your life becomes more satisfying to you and others, if your life works with a new ease and excitement, if barriers fall away, if opportunities open up, if life is a series of 'yes' signs—you know your guiding images are being fulfilled. You are synchronizing yourself with the best opportunities both for your inner self and for the universe. Mostly, of course, this synchronization happens with others who share your dreams.

Here is a recent example of synchronization in my own life. I awoke one morning with a dream that symbolically told me not to continue putting effort into a foundation I had established. I had been able to get nonprofit status for it, but that turned out to mean getting about 20,000 dollars in debt. Perhaps I should give the foundation to someone better qualified to carry out its goals of research? I asked one parapsychologist if she was interested. No, she had just investigated the legalities of such a situation and concluded it was not for her. My wife suggested that I call Jeffrey Mishlove, who had recently received his doctorate in parapsychology and had worked with me to establish a library for consciousness research.

As I reached for the telephone to call Mishlove in San Francisco, the telephone rang. It was Mishlove calling me—for the first time since I had moved to Los Angeles—to tell me that he and his wife were moving into a nice large house.

'Would you like a foundation to go with the house?' I asked. Of course he would. He would be able to maintain the library in this large house, which even had a special room in which seminars could be held. Our dreams seemed to be synchronized.

When feedback from the universe assumes a *negative* character, the message is: 'Rethink your goals and strategy.' We learn more from our mistakes than from our successes, so pay attention to those 'no' signs. They may, in fact, even be generated by your inner self to influence your environment to tell you that you are doing the wrong thing. Or that you may have the right plan but the wrong opportunity.

The latter seemed to be evident when I recently experienced a remarkable series of dissynchronizations, or 'no' signs. I had moved to Los Angeles from San Francisco because of a series of dreams that told me I must get involved in the media. The dream even spelled out my area code of 213 for Los Angeles. Everything went smoothly in the move and I found just the right house in two days, so that part of my life change seemed synchronized with my inner self.

My first opportunities for television appearances came soon after. Two producers from two new television shows somehow heard of me and asked me to appear on their shows. I visited one producer and talked with the other and hoped that we would be able to work something out. After all, I had come to

Los Angeles specifically for such opportunities.

But my universe seemed to disagree: in the same day, two of my tooth caps broke off while I was vigorously flossing, two supports in my favorite chair broke and I had to throw it out, and twice a cabinet on the wall came crashing down. I just couldn't help noticing the coincidence of those 'no' signs. I did not pursue the shows any further. When I finally saw them, I was grateful I had no connection with them. Both shows were terrible, I thought.

Opportunity for a nationwide television show finally came when I was ready, and manifested the positive synchronicity I was looking for. One evening I got a call from a talk-show producer, who asked me to substitute for another psychic. I was stunned when I heard the psychic's name. At that very moment I was reading a book about him and his many media appearances, and wondering how he made the contacts. Now I had one of my own. The recommendation to call me had come from an associate producer with whom I had worked on another kind of project altogether. Again, the Small World Effect. My appearance on the show went well.

Society's Guiding Images

To discover society's collective dreams—the guiding images that we share—we must become the prophets of a new order. We must use our creative consciousness to become the science-fiction writers of reality. It might help to find out how science-fiction writers create their best worlds. Here is a tip from science-fiction editor and writer Ben Bova:

> To show other worlds, to describe possible future societies and the problems lurking ahead, is not enough. The writer of science fiction *must show how these worlds and these futures affect human beings.* And something much more important: *He must show how human beings can and do literally create these future worlds.* For our future is largely in our hands. It doesn't come blindly rolling out of the heavens; it is the joint product of the actions of billions of human beings. This is a point that's easily forgotten in the rush of headlines and the hectic badgering of everyday life. But it's a point that science fiction makes constantly: The future belongs to us—whatever it is. We make it; our actions shape tomorrow. We have the brains and guts to build paradise (or at least try). Tragedy is when we fail, and the greatest crime of all is when we fail even to try.[52]

The prophetic visions of science-fiction are seldom of paradise. As our society's visionaries, science-fiction writers and filmmakers often offer us negative images of tomorrow. They do this in the manner of a chiding parent who warns his or her offspring that the worst will happen if he continues acting the way he does. But just as sure as you tell a child never to stuff a bean up his nose, that child will stuff a bean up his nose. Negative warnings, prophesies of doom, scary tales of a future society gone mad, of scientific catastrophe and human debasement achieve the opposite of what their prophets hoped for.

Our consciousness is far more impressionable than most people realize. Studies of the effects of heavy media publicity in murder-suicides show a significant rise in accidental deaths on the highways and among pilots of small planes. Once implanted in our minds, negative suggestions can take over without our realizing it. Violence is a virulent disease that spreads from consciousness to consciousness. Negative expectations, pessimism, fear, and terror likewise spread like a contagion that infects a whole society. Negative visions characterize the expectations of our age.

Prophets of doom sell millions of copies of their books and cassettes. They have millions of followers who expect the worse, and in a perverse way look forward to Armageddon. This attitude stops progress in its tracks. As one observer put it, 'You don't polish brass on a sinking ship.' Why bother trying to improve things if it's all going to blow up anyway? Others head for the hills and stock up on provisions—and guns to keep away the city folk when Armageddon comes.

Yet there *are* visionaries of a positive future for us. Their books don't sell millions, their ideas are sometimes far-fetched or so they seem to mainstream folks, their writings appear in small publications like *The Futurist*, they have societies, like the World Future Society, they have meetings, they disseminate ideas about the future, they try to create a better future. Their day is coming soon.

Veteran future watcher Roy Amara, president of the Institute for the Future, in Menlo Park, California, characterizes those who best generate positive guiding images of the future as 'visionaries, mavericks, or even geniuses. Such individuals possess a keen ability to view the world in unconventional and innovative ways that stimulate, educate, and stretch the mind. They tend to be intuitive and feeling in their thought processes and are effective writers who can communicate with mass audiences.'[53]

Think of visionaries of the past: Thomas Edison, a maverick genius without formal schooling who prophesied light; Dale Carnegie, who prophesied how to win friends and influence people; Bishop Fulton J. Sheen, who prophesied peace of soul to millions on television; and Norman Vincent Peale, who still prophesies the power of positive thinking.

A whole new generation of visionaries will find an audience for their positive visions of a society that works for everyone. Replacing the cult of the self as center will be new philosophies embracing the society as opportunity for all.

If our collective vision of the future should be guided by our collective inner selves, we may discover that the diverse segments of our society agree on more things than they disagree on. I foresee a time coming soon when the dominant social attitude will shift from 'I want my share' to 'Let me share with you, so that you can share with me.' We will become intently aware of being in this — 'this' being the future — together. As our government's social programs are dropped (which I predicted in 1979), communities will band together to help their people in ways that will prove much better for us than the old method of government handouts. A new sense of community sharing and closeness will develop.

We shall see the beginnings of a new style of social consciousness in which we will overcome our greatest problems by giving our young people the opportunity to fulfill their potentials. The old-style thinking, exemplified by fighting crime by building more prisons and employing more police, will give way to a more enlightened thinking that will help would-be criminals find meaning in their lives through their own creativity.

We are, at present, an imbalanced society in treacherous waters. Most of our attempts to right the balance are, as one wag said, 'like rearranging the deck chairs on the *Titanic*'. We are not getting to the core of our problems because society does not yet realize that only through future vision can we achieve that balance. We must all become visionaries to foresee that the best guiding images of society are those that, in the long run, give us *all* a chance.

We must ask of our society the same questions we ask of ourselves: What if I foresee how I can make things work better? Will I take steps to make it that way?

As a visionary friend of mine says, 'Getting the vision is easy. It's making it come true that's the hard part.'

Let us take Ben Bova's advice on creating the future and 'show how human beings can and do literally create these future worlds'.

If we can see that future, we can believe it. Let us find those who share our vision and work to make our dreams come true.

Exercises

See the Goal

1. Before you go to bed at night, think about the things you have to do tomorrow. If some particular task or challenge comes to mind, see yourself in your mind's eye already having accomplished it. You see and hear applause from others because you did so well. They are cheering you. You take a bow. You are relaxed and confident because you knew all along you could do it well. Linger on the feeling of satisfaction.

2. The next day, after you have accomplished your goal, compare your actual feelings with those you experienced in your prevision. If you feel satisfaction, you have learned how to see the goal.

3. Repeat this regularly for about a minute each night before you go to bed or before some challenging task.

4. If feedback from your universe is positive, you are learning how to shape your future. If feedback is negative, you may be trying too hard. Relax and don't push; just let it happen.

Fulfilling a Guiding Image

1. Select from your list of guiding images one that could be put into action now. It could be anything from communicating better with your spouse to writing a magazine article.

2. Now relax and see in your mind's eye an image of the results of your fulfilling that goal. Think of the last time you were successful at a similar task and recreate that feeling of satisfaction. Let the image and feeling of satisfaction stay in your consciousness for about a minute. See yourself being applauded for doing so well. You know it will be easy because you have seen it happen. Your spouse is happy at the attention you are giving your family and is returning your communication; your magazine editor is delighted to see your manuscript and is writing you a check.

3. If any ideas or action came while you were visualizing your guiding image, use it as a first step toward making your goal happen. Think of something interesting to tell your spouse; take a piece of paper and put on it a title for your magazine article.

4. Every day for the next few days, visualize your goal for one minute and feel confident that it will happen. Follow your spontaneous impulses. You might suggest to your spouse an evening on the town; you might write a lead for your magazine article.

5. Ask yourself if there is anything standing in the way of your goal that you can remove by your actions. You might give your spouse a book to read that you enjoyed so you will have something to discuss; you might do more research for your article to become an authority on the subject.

6. When the time seems right, complete your goal and get feedback on your success. You might spend a whole evening talking with your spouse about your relationship; you might complete your article and send it to the editor.

7. Afterwards, compare your initial visualization with what actually happened. Did your spouse confide in you? Did your editor like your article and send you a check?

8. If the goal was not achieved, try again. Make a greater effort to communicate with your spouse; write a new magazine article and send the first one to another magazine editor.

9. Keep up your visualizations for as long as it takes to accomplish your goal. If the goal is a true guiding image, it will be fulfilled—sooner than you may think.

12.

Time Will Tell

Time, like space, has always seemed to most people like such a constant thing. Clocks, chronometers, celestial timekeepers like the sun and the moon, with their regularity, make us aware of an eternal rhythm. We set our electronic watches to the second, we synchronize our lives to time, and it all seems to work.

We become aware of different kinds of time. A moment in a dentist's chair stretches out to seem longer than an entire night spent in a lover's embrace. That's psychological time, we tell ourselves; the differences are only an illusion.

When Albert Einstein introduced the concept of relative time and space, he shocked the scientific community. Experiment showed that time is distorted by speed and mass, and we comforted ourselves with the notion that that sort of thing doesn't happen here on earth. It only happens out there, in the vast reaches of the heavens, and perhaps in those mysterious theoretical entities known as black holes. A black hole, we are chilled to learn, is so massive that it squeezes the space and time out of matter.

The beginning of the universe is just as bothersome for our concepts of space and time. Astronomers have tracked the radiation from the initial Big Bang that created space, time and matter in an instant. We cannot speak of *before* that instant because there was no time. We can speak only of the universe being born in a cosmic explosion about 15 billion years ago. It comes as a surprise to most of us that space and time are still being created on the edges of the universe.

When I try to conceive of how this enormous universe of galaxies, nebulas, stars and planets came out of nothing, my head hurts. When I try to understand how time, space and matter were instantaneously created, my headache worsens. My logical mind just cannot conceive of all this. So I have to turn the problem over to my intuitive mind, and see what happens.

Here is the picture I get: almost like the biblical story of creation, a consciousness outside of space and time conceived of a universe and brought it into being in an instant. He (that cosmic consciousness) gave his own qualities to this new universe of space time and matter. It, like He, is holographic: the world is contained in each of its parts; each part can reconstruct the whole.

The universe was born with a purpose, a destiny. What seem like random events in the enormity of time have, in reality, direction and purpose. For one thing, they enabled us—human beings—to be created in the image of the cosmic consciousness. We, like He, have individual destinies. We, too, have a purpose; we, too, create our own universes; we, too, create space, time, and matter.

In order to create time, we do not have to know a whit of theory. We need only consciousness, which selects which probability will come into reality. We influence random events to line up in the long run according to will. Our mind force not only influences reality, but, collectively, *creates* it.

Suppose that this is so. Does it give us any advantage in living our lives? Can this knowledge, if it is true, enhance the ways in which we might fulfill our destinies?

Consider this idea. The way we experience time is the perception of a collection of events: the faster events are experienced, the more time seems speeded up; when events come slowly, our sense of time is slowed. If, for example, you are watching cars go by, and a hundred come and go in an hour, you experience a rapid passage of time. If only one car comes by, you sense a slow passage of time. The experience of time is relative to the number of events.

If we foresee a distant goal and focus our mind powers to achieve that goal, our success will depend on how many events we can influence. If you want to have a baby by next week, for example, all of your concentration will not help. If you want that baby within five years, you have a good chance, because there are thousands and thousands more random events that you can influence. And, of course, because it takes a gestation period for the baby.

If our consciousness foresees a future event, that very act of precognition makes the event more likely. When we touch things with our minds, we change them. Physicists speak of the 'observer effect' to mean the same thing on the quantum level. I suggest it happens also in our daily lives. When we observe things in the future with our minds, we are helping to create them. We self-fulfill our prophecies.

So when you foresee a baby within five years, your very act of prevision influences you to make it happen. That shouldn't be too much of a surprise. We are always planning future events—seeing them in our minds—and then taking action to bring them about. The surprise may come when we consider that the further away our goal is in time, the better chance we will have to accomplish it.

The elevator experiment cited in Chapter 3 gives some evidence for this idea. The subject got his highest scoring rate (77 per cent) when he was trying to predict over the greatest period of time (16 hours). I think his very act of prediction influenced the future arrival times of the elevator; the more events that could be influenced over time, the better his success.

But did you ever say, 'I don't want to think about the future. I don't have time to cope with the present.' We all have said that at certain points in our lives, usually at desperate moments. Mostly, they came about because we had not thought about the future before them. Because we did not exercise our gift of foresight (or prevision) in the past, we pay in the present with a feeling of panic and inability to cope. We get caught up in the problems of the present and tend to exclude from our thoughts the very necessary prevision of the future that will lessen our problems later. The next time you get caught up in the feeling of not wanting to know the future, consider that by wanting to know, you can actually improve the future. The future is not something that happens by itself.

I have already suggested that we create time. Now I suggest that we create the future. If you think about it, those statements are really identical. The future consists of time units, of a measuring of events, and the events in turn are selected by our consciousness. But since each of us experiences his or her personal universe a little differently, each of us creates time a little differently. We express our individual personalities in the creation of time and the future.

That statement may seem shocking to those who regard time as a constant. But the evidence is compelling. Although the greater universal consciousness (as far as we can surmise) *collectively* creates a framework of time and space, we, as individuals, create our *individual* universes of time and space. We foresee events in different ways; express our individuality through precognition.

We can foresee events both in our lives and in the lives of others. There is, however, a difference between the two experiences. When we prevision events in our own lives, we tend to make them happen; we are the primary psychic observers who influence those events. When we foresee events in someone else's life, we are, like viewers of a movie, not responsible for their creation; we are secondary observers. It may be quite true that we exert *some* small influence, but it is miniscule compared to that of the author of the life events we foresee. It is a difference that assumes importance when we think about premonitions. If I foresee the crash of an airplane or an assassination, I am no more responsible than a moviegoer watching such an event on the screen. But if I foresee an event in my own life, I am involved: it is my movie and I have the final cut. The responsibility is mine.

What happens when many people foresee the same event? If the event is a large-scale happening that could affect the lives of all in the group, the future event will tend to happen. If millions upon millions of people foresee the same outcome, it helps that future to happen. The influence of television may be paramount in influencing public events. If people are not only alerted to a possible future but are given actual images of it to help their own efforts at prevision, it becomes easier for them to see it happen. The future of space flight involves them all. The advent of space technologies becomes a global phenomenon that effects the future of the whole human race, so everyone assumes some responsibility for that future.

If that is true, so are the negative possibilities. If many millions of television viewers are alerted to the possibility of an Armageddon, and are given images of that terrible future to help them prevision it, it will tend to happen. War is a powerful archetype of the collective consciousness; it needs only a minimum amount of psychic prevision to activate it, and once activated it tends toward completion.

Societal futures, both positive and negative, seem to be out of our individual control. Each of us contributes to those futures, yes, but in such a small proportion that it becomes frustrating to attempt any influence over such massive events. The best thing to do is to concentrate our previsionary abilities and our life's energy to select our own best possible futures with the knowledge that if we live our lives abundantly we shall contribute to an abundant society.

If we as individuals experience success in foreseeing and fulfilling our best futures, we gain confidence that the same techniques can be used in our communities. Once we understand how to make our own lives work better, we will be better prepared to make society work better. Once we have the experience, we can work together to achieve a mutual resonance of vision and the will to accomplish our collective goals.

It is my belief that we can achieve our utopias *only* by developing our individual talents for creating a better future. We do not fulfill our collective destinies by accident, but rather by applying our godlike powers of mind. We shape tomorrow from the fabric of our inner destinies with the tools of our creative consciousness.

Is it True?

Is there any way of testing what I have said? Can scientific experiment determine if my theory is true or if it is just one of hundreds of untestable theories proposed over the millennia? Many modern theorists of precognition and psychic phenomena have offered explanations, models, insights, have described psychic processes, and have made many contributions to understanding psychic functioning at several levels. But they have not proposed a testable theory. They have not yet offered a theory comparable to Einstein's simple but fundamental equation of $e = mc^2$.

Well, I don't claim to have outdone Einstein, but I do have a testable theory. It may be right; it may be wrong. But at least scientific experiment can find the truth. And if it is true, it might have far-reaching possibilities of application. Recall that Einstein's simple equation of $e = mc^2$ made possible the development of atomic energy.

My basic statement of reality is not an equation, but has to do with relationships of relativity. Time is relative to human consciousness; space is relative to human consciousness; matter is relative to human consciousness. The success of human consciousness in creating space, time, and matter is relative to the available number of events it can foresee and influence.[54]

I have proposed a dozen experimental tests of this theory. The basic idea for these laboratory tests is that space, time and matter will vary according to psychological variables of the subjects in psychic testing; and that the results should not be affected by pre-existing parameters of space, time, and matter.

Recent experiments in psychokinesis at Princeton University have confirmed one of my experimental predictions—that each person should display a unique 'mindprint' in psychokinesis experiments. The principal experimenters, Robert G. John and Brenda Dunne, discovered just such 'mind prints' that identify each subject's data.[55]

In matters of prevision, and providing we will be given feedback for an event in our future, the theory predicts that our success at seeing through time will tend to improve with the greater number of events that will contribute to the final outcome; and that, conversely, so-called time constants will not affect our success. If, for example, I try to predict the colour of the one thousandth car that will drive by, my success will not be dependent on whether that happens in a week, a month, or a year, so long as I am there to see the car drive by and know it's the target car. If the cars come by at a constant rate, my chances for success will actually improve with time; my prediction, say, of a brown car to be the one thousandth may actually influence the driver of a brown car to fulfill my prediction. The more cars available for influencing, the better my chances of success.

In the laboratory it would be electronic devices that generate the targets. And because electronic events happen by the billions, they are more easily foreseen and influenced: when we observe them in the future, we, by that very action, tend to influence them.

The aspect of the theory that has the greatest potential for application resides in the holographic (or holonomic) nature of consciousness. Each of us possesses a fragmentary piece of the collective consciousness of the universe. So we potentially have access to all knowledge of the universe, albeit in fuzzy and fragmentary form. The Mobius Society has already demonstrated that individual respondents to psychic questions answer imperfectly, but that when their statements are examined for consensus, a more accurate and dependable answer emerges. The technique is also being used by William H. Kautz at the Center for Applied Intuition near San Francisco.

This technique can be improved upon, I believe, when individual psychics are brought together in groups so that their consciousness can unite into a collective field. The more pieces of a holographic structure that are joined together, the greater the definition and clarity of their collective vision. The techniques needed to achieve this collective psychic vision will not be difficult to develop. Several experiments have successfully used groups united in their consciousness to achieve a collective result far more accurate than that of any one individual.

Time will tell if my theory and its possible applications will lead to the development of holographic consciousness technlogy. If I do my job as prophet well, and many others begin to envision a future enhanced by consciousness technology, we stand a better chance for making that dream come true. To improve my odds for success, I shall devote the last chapter to prophesies of fulfillment through consciousness technology. I'm betting that many of you will recognize some of your own guiding images in my future vision of the third millennium's beginning.

Human Destiny

Where is the human race going and how will we get there? Do we have within our collective psyches blueprints of our ultimate destiny?

Those are questions modern-day science cannot answer. Most scientists do not even think the questions have any meaning. They think we are just a fortunate accident that happened by a series of longshots throughout the enormity of time. And so any future for us would also be a series of accidents, for materialistic science has no concept of consciousness creating its own reality.

Yet there are, I believe, scientific principles at work in forming our destiny. And it is even part of our destiny to discover those principles and utilize them to hasten our voyage through time and space. When we become historians of our past, we see the roots of our future. Human beings have an urge to explore, colonize, and explore some more. We are always seeking new frontiers to conquer and make in our image.

Our psychic heritage from millions of years ago will not quietly disappear now that opportunities for terrestrial exploration and colonization have petered out. The urge is too strong. We are like salmon that must seek their breeding place to spawn a new generation. We will not rest until we plant our seed in the stars, for it is *out there* that the universe began, it is out there that *we* began, along with all the rest of creation, and it is our destiny to find our home in the stars.

How will we do this? Our scientists tell us that the speed of light is the absolute speed limit of the universe. The vast reaches of the stars are so far by our terrestrial standards that we cannot even comprehend that kind of distance.

But if I am right in saying that we create time and space, the problem of traversing great spans of time and space changes to the problem of how to create space-time so that we can be where we desire. We do not traverse anything—we are just suddenly there. To master that ultimate technique of space-time teleportation, we must first master our own consciousness. And this will necessarily entail our working together on a profound level of meshed consciousness that can achieve results undreamed of for an individual.

If this sounds like science fiction, it may be because science-fiction writers are tapping the same collective dream of humankind's destiny. If it seems impossible today, that is only because we have not yet seen it so that we can believe it.

Let's consider the earlier stages of human evolution that might lead to such an extraordinary development that now seems so impossible. To do so, we must have an insight into the nature of human evolution. Human beings are the quintessence of computer capability. Our exquisite circuitry is programmed with a highly complex series of instructions. We can see this most clearly in the development of a fetus and in early childhood, when changes come so quickly. Each programmed stage must be reached before the next circuit goes into operation. We speak of developmental stages. But potential circuits of the brain are there, waiting for the right signal to put them into operation. This development process does not stop when adulthood is reached, it only slows. Whether or not additional circuits are triggered into operation depends not so much on the signals from the glands but on the mental preparation of the adult. If an individual pushes his or her capabilities to their extreme, he or she automatically triggers the next circuit's operation.

That is a computerese way of saying that we possess potentials for genius that can be achieved only by trying. And the type of genius I'm talking about is achieving mastery over space, time, and matter as well as the more conventional notion of being a brilliant thinker and problem-solver.

If we are created in the image of God or the cosmic consciousness, the evidence is that God must be the ultimate computer—going far beyond our limited concepts of what a computer can do. As further evidence, we have the urge to create beings in our own image—and create computers. They are getting better all the time. When we imbue them with human personality, we call them robots. Our film-maker visionaries have given us Hal (in *2001: A Space Odyssey*). R2D2 and C3PO (in *Star Wars*), and endless numbers of spinoffs both malevolent and cute, in other movies and TV productions. Our scientists are not far behind.

The movie robot-computers capture our imagination because they satisfy our urge to create beings in our own image. When those fantasies become a reality, you can be sure that our robots of the future will indeed have personalities.

The future development of robotics will be tied in with our own development. As we open up new circuitry, we will pass on to them the latest capabilities we have discovered. We may even succeed in imbuing our future robots with an intelligence that surpasses that of anyone living today. Those future robots will help us build new technologies that will be linked with our own minds to achieve extraordinary control over space, time, and matter.

Once we achieve that control, we shall be on our destined ways to the stars in search of our maker. What we shall find may surpass the fantasies of science fiction. Arthur C. Clarke, in *Childood's End*, speaks of our destiny to join the Overmind. Clarke is only spinning a tale of fantasy, he says. But many other tales of fantasy have come true. This one, I believe, will happen before the dawn of the fourth millennium on 1 January 3001.

Time will tell.

Exercises

Guiding Images of Society

1.   Select from your guiding images one that could benefit society as a whole.
2.   In your's mind's eye, imagine how that guiding image might be accomplished. Would it take co-operation from other people?
3.   Ask some friends to your house for a goal party. Tell them that they will have a chance to express their hopes for the future and for society. Tell the group of your goal for yourself and for society. Then ask each person to tell what their goal might be.
4.   If there are any similarities or dovetailing of goals, encourage discussion between people who share the same vision. You may find someone who shares your dream.
5.   Ask the group if anyone has been able to achieve a similar goal in the past. How did he or she do it? You may get some good ideas.
6.   If you or others find you share some goals, arrange to get together more frequently to discuss ways of helping each other accomplish the goal. It would be best if the whole group can agree on a single goal.
7.   Think about your goal every day and visualize it being fulfilled for about a minute. In your visualization you may sense some inspiration of how to accomplish it.

8. When you meet again with the others who share your goal, mention any ideas or inspirations you may have. See if the others have any new ideas. Talk about them.

9. If your sharing of information with others has produced some plan of action to accomplish your goal, consider that the plan could start with you.

10. If there is some small thing that could be done to get a little closer to your goal for yourself and society, find a way to begin. You may find that you can begin with the help of the others.

11. After you take the first step, you may find that you have ideas for further steps.

12. Take one step at a time.

13.

2001: A Prophetic Odyssey

In the dawn of the third millennium lies the most powerful technology ever devised: the technology of human consciousness. Once we accept responsibility for our future realities and achieve a profound belief in our godlike powers of mind, the sky is not the limit—it is only the beginning.

The years approaching the third millennium may be the most crucial era in our history. In that crucible of challenges will be forged not only a new will to make the future work but the beginnings of a new era of human evolution. It will not be easy. Prophets of doom sap our will and darken our vision of the future. The precipice of disaster seems to loom ever closer with each new report of war and rumor of war. Much of the world is fearful. Staring into the faces of the horsemen of the Apocalypse, some are hypnotized with terror and surrender hope.

Perhaps we have reached the bottom of Pandora's box. After the evil forces have been unleashed in our world, when we are despairing, we find hope.

Join me in a prophetic odyssey to the advent of the third millennium. It begins on 1 January 2001. As we celebrate the new year, the new century, the new millennium, will we also celebrate the condition of the human race? Time will tell. And it will tell the most to those who have foreseen it. Listen to your own intuitions, your own hearts, and judge if my prophecies of the dawning of an era of consciousness technology will become a dream of promise for our collective future. It can happen only if you believe it can. It can happen only if you, too, foresee it. It can happen only if you share that dream and act to make it come true.

Prologue

The last years of the second millennium are turbulent, filled with anxiety and unrest. The U.S. Government has reacted to fears of economic depression by wildly manipulating currency and interest rates in hopes of achieving a balanced economy. World-wide economic instability threatens the collapse of the economies of several nations. But major gains have been made in reducing nuclear weapons. Soviet and American *rapprochement* has risen to new heights, and now focuses on what can be done in the economic arena to help collapsing countries.

The truth about the classified 'ESP War' that took place in the mid-80s between the Soviet Union and United States now emerges and reveals that most of the secret work was bungled. Yet one positive development comes as researchers learn how to enhance intuitive/psychic abilities in training programs for government and industry. Ten per cent of people who take this training learn fair control over their intuitive abilities. And one per cent of these become quite proficient in their use of consciousness technology. It is this one per cent who become leaders in advancing a new consciousness based on creating a future based on both science and intuition.

Education

High-school and college students are being taught how to balance their left and right-brain functions with biofeedback devices. Students are learning to use their intuition and ESP in problem solving along with logic to find the answers that work best. Enhanced brain functioning combined with advanced techniques in learning enable students to memorize in an hour what formerly took a week. Emphasis on learning shifts to creative thinking and learning how to learn. Renewed interest in the creative arts accompanies this new approach. The performing arts, writing, music, art, dance and other esthetic pursuits find a strong place in the curriculum.

Vocational counselors for young people now use psychic and consciousness techniques to help students make the right career choices. Vocational training begins in high school, especially for students whose talents lie in practical areas. Under the supervision of retired experts in many career areas, young people who formerly dropped out now receive pay for training and working in special apprenticeship programs financed by local communities.

Many students are opening up their own small businesses and learning how to be productive. Financing for these businesses comes from local communities, which also supply retired businessmen as advisers to keep the students on track. The retirees derive great satisfaction from their productive work, and some become senior partners with the young businessmen.

Special programs are enacted for the academically gifted so that these students can develop to the height of their potential. Their innovative contributions to society have already made the program pay for itself.

Crime

Due to the burgeoning opportunites now open to young people, there are fewer school dropouts and bitter youths trying to get back at society by committing crime. Urban street gangs have nearly vanished. Youths are finding productive and satisfying work in small business and shops financed by community loans. Fewer police are needed in urban areas.

Police recruits are routinely tested for psychic ability. Those who show unusual talent are trained to use their abilities to increase the efficiency of crime detection and enforcement. Criminals are quickly apprehended with these psychic techniques. When hardened criminals learn how easily they can be caught, many of them decide to try some safer occupation.

Criminals who are sent to prison receive intensive rehabilitation through consciousness techniques that help them realize that they can make their lives what they want them to be. Parole officers have helped paroled prisoners find satisfying careers in special programs financed by the states. Many parolees are paid to learn new vocations, and those who want to start their own businesses are lent state funds. Criminal recidivism dramatically drops, and states find that they are spending far less money in their new programs than they spent on housing prisoners.

During their prison stays, criminals have opportunities to develop their psychic talents; they become aware that if they harm others, they are harming themselves. After release some ex-convicts become leaders in their communities, some work with the police in inspiring young offenders to leave lives of crime for productive and satisfying work in the community.

Energy

Oil companies are regularly using psychic and consciousness techniques to improve their chances of success in the exploration and drilling of new wells. Where formerly they found oil only 10 per cent of the time, now 60 per cent is considered acceptable. This 500 per cent increase in efficiency has lowered the price of gas and oil, and provided new funds for research into alternative energies and better use of conventional fuels

As the new energy research programs begin to pay off, the oil demand lessens, and oil companies change their names to energy companies as their new investments in alternative energies bring greater income than oil.

When consciousness techniques are applied to the development of nuclear fusion power plants, nuclear fusion becomes a cheap, reliable, and safe method of producing electricity. The old atomic power plants are replaced by fusion plants to meet increased energy needs.

The Arms Race

The Soviet-American disarmament plan, begun in talks in 1987, goes into force. Both superpowers begin to dismantle nuclear missiles. When an atomic device is exploded in the Middle East, the United States and the Soviet Union are spurred to disarm all nuclear weapons and establish an international nuclear arms regulatory commission to ban nuclear weapons in all countries. Equipped with a few nuclear missiles to enforce the ban, the United Nations Nuclear Arms Regulatory Commission uses psychic techniques to insure that no secret bombs are built by any country.

Now that world tension is lessened, the United States and the Soviet Union agree to reduce their military budgets by 5 per cent each year. Half of the money saved goes to the United Nations, half to the economies of their own countries. In the Soviet Union people who were trained to become psychics during the ESP war developed visionary qualities and are now demanding that their government's money be put to use in building a better society. The Soviets make swift progress under the tutelage of the ESP war veterans trained in consciousness techniques.

Science

Think tanks begin using consciousness techniques to speed up scientific progress. A team of scientists and psychics at a California think tank discover the principles of antigravity, and the first manned flight to Mars is planned using antigravity propulsion systems. Since the new system does not need rockets, the astronauts can use a space shuttle that is already built; they equip it with the simple antigravity device and slowly take off. As a Soviet-American team leaves the atmosphere, their speed increases to a hundred times that of rocket ships. Their landing on Mars is as gentle as their takeoff, and their return trip is easier than that of the first space shuttle. They don't have to glide through the atmosphere; they float down.

Long-standing plans for a space station in orbit around the earth are now activated. With the antigravity propulsion system it becomes easy, fast and relatively cheap to transport material into space. Refined radio telescopes detect signals from extraterrestrials when guided to the proper co-ordinates by teams of psychics. The psychics help decode the transmission, and contact with other minds begins.

New breakthroughs in science and technology accelerate as think tanks become more skilled in the use of consciousness technology to solve long-standing problems.

Medicine

Medicine begins to make widespread use of biofeedback techniques coupled with consciousness techniques to treat progressive diseases such as cancer. As more people realize the role of their own consciousness in producing disease, doctors made use of consciousness techniques to help patients heal themselves without surgery or drugs.

The emphasis of medicine is now to prevent disease. Using psychic treatment techniques, doctors become skilled in treating their patients with what used to be called the 'placebo effect'. Regular counseling sessions with patients while they are well dramatically reduces the incidence of disease.

Medical schools introduce short (three-year) programs for lay doctors who are trained primarily in patient care and teaching patients how to heal themselves. Many nurses opt to become lay doctors, actively promoting healing by consciousness techniques and counseling preventative medicine. More than 80 per cent of patients who paid for regular doctor care in the past now find that lay doctors are cheaper and more effective in dealing with their common ailments. Many minority people become lay doctors and start programs in ghetto areas, ushering in a revolution in health care for the poor.

The dramatic drop in hard-core patients needing expert medical care releases more M.D.s to do medical research, which is funded by the new health care plans that are now making money. The new preventative medicine techniques become so effective that the cost of medical care plummets.

Medical schools now have courses in psychic diagnosis, which speeds up the diagnostic process. Medical research teams utilize consciousness techniques to come up with improved treatment and breakthrough cures for formerly incurable diseases, such as muscular dystrophy.

The common cold becomes a rarity as more and more people adopt the self-preventative technique of 10 minutes of self-healing each day to keep themselves healthy. Their improved immune system proves more resistant to common ailments.

Research into AIDS begins using intuitive techniques to find a vaccine that prevents the AIDS virus from multiplying. Researchers find that people who practice self-healing are much more resistant to the outbreak of AIDS-related diseases.

Government

Pressure from citizens who have learned consciousness techniques exerts enough influence to put into party platforms the promise that the best futurist/psychic consultations will be sought before major programs are budgeted.

Many people still feel the old way may be best for government, but a growing number of voters want to see psychic probes done on the candidates to find out if they are telling the truth and will fulfill their promises.

A growing grass-roots community movement wants tax dollars to go directly to the local communities rather than to the federal government. A compromise is reached in which federal taxes are reduced by half, so that local communities can raise money through income taxes. The community income taxes are lower, however, and more money stays in the taxpayer's pockets. Federal government programs are slashed, and the local communities take over their functions. Taxes become lower as the effects of decreases in the military budget are felt.

Government at all levels becomes more efficient and less costly as consciousness techniques are routinely used to aid in making decisions and solving problems.

By the year 2001 the federal government has substantially

reduced its budgetary needs—since so much tax money goes directly to the communities without going through federal bureaus—that it has decreased in size and its responsibility for domestic programs. More and more, the country is running itself.

The U.S. president is no longer regarded as a celebrity but more like the chairman of the board, who keeps a low profile and spends his time making decisions. Foreign policy now becomes the president's chief responsibility. His work is made easier by teams of psychics and consciousness researchers who monitor foreign developments with such accuracy that foreign countries now realize they can no longer keep secrets from us, and we realize that soon we will not be able to keep secrets from them.

The Economy

The national economy has improved in many areas by the widespread use of consciousness technology. In this era of abundance the United States is able to invest more in foreign countries, and they too, under the tutelage of American psychic advisers, improve their productivity and economic base.

The increase in productivity has lessened inflation and made more money available for new investment. Interest rates have fallen as money becomes easily obtainable for loans. The first major effect is felt in the housing industry, as cheap loans spur construction of new housing.

Industry

Industrial corporations are among the first to make use of consciousness technology. Before tooling up for new, costly designs of major goods, they use psychic probes to find out how the public will react to their new designs. Using consciousness market research they obtain information about what the public will want, and then produce it. Better sales and fewer unwanted creations make for strong growth of industry.

Industrial engineers use consciousness technology to dream up highly efficient and cheaply produced innovations in many areas. Household robots are on the market. Hand-held computers are produced for school children and adults, who are learning sophisticated computer techniques for everyday application. Many industrial workers now work from home at their computer consoles, which are linked in to the main office.

By the year 2001 many corporations are using computerized

automation in turning out new products. Former assembly-line workers now run machines, perform quality control, and use consciousness technology to refine manufacturing processes. Workers, with the aid of computer technology, become more efficient and need work only four days a week, many on their own schedules.

Companies now regularly send their management trainees to learn consciousness techniques at special academies. The trainees learn how to balance their brain functioning by using intuition and ESP along with logic to make the best decisions. Those who show the greatest intuitive talent climb the corporate ladder more quickly, and many become presidents of companies at an early age.

The Arts and the Media

The performing arts are beginning a renaissance that continues unabated into the year 2001. A significant by-product of the consciousness techniques taught in schools is the enhancement and development of artistic talent. Many young people discover talents they didn't know they had, even a significant number of adults are encouraged to dust off half-forgotten skills and talents. Everyone, it seems, has the need toward self-expression through music, dance, theater and art. Community groups spring up around the country as local showcases for the performing arts.

Amateur filmmaking becomes the rage as new technical processes make it possible for the average person to afford equipment to make three-reel movies. Writers, directors, actors and other film contributors are found at community performing arts groups. Amateur film festivals become a popular pastime, as a new generation of film directors is born. People who used to show slides of their vacation trips now show their latest movies, some of which are good.

Hollywood movie studios, threatened by the competition, decide to finance certain talented amateur filmmakers to make professional-quality but low-budget movies that can be shown for less money than studio-produced films. Too many Hollywood blockbuster movies have gone bust, and tastes have changed; people look for creative, imaginative and artistically produced products that inspire them to improve their own movies.

The explosion in amateur filmmaking spills over to television. Already beset by declining revenues because the public no longer wants the old formulas, the television industry looks for new products to match the new temper of the times. Now, instead of a malady-of-the-month movie, TV shows the most-creative-new-filmmaker movie of the month. More and more independent stations are taking away the markets of the major networks. These new stations are more innovative and offer opportunities for new filmmakers and others who show creative talent.

Television's soap operas are vanishing as daytime audiences discover it is more fun to make up and act in their own dramas than watching them on TV. Many former addicts of the soaps are now taking to writing their own episodes with their favorite characters and adding new characters from their own lives. Improvisational soap opera becomes a big hit at the community playhouses.

Music is showing an astonishing diversity as new forms and instruments are combined with the human voice to achieve moving effects on listeners. The latest wave is combining some of the rock 'n' roll sounds of the sixties with gospel style lyrics to celebrate life in songs that inspire the audience to sing along. Sing-ins become a popular entertainment as more people become aware of the power of music to unite them in a single feeling and purpose. Some progressive churches begin to substitute this new wave for traditional hymns. The new wave songs seem to sing themselves, expressing harmonically the richness of group feeling.

Pictorial art and sculpture take on a mystical quality. Using newly developed pigments that glow and shimmer, experimental artists create canvases of abstract yet strangely human forms, which have a joyous effect on the viewers. The newest form of art is light-painting, in which multi-colored lasers are programmed by computer to make intricate, feathery designs in the night. Several banks and hotels now have nightly programs of light-painting that can be seen from the tops of their towers and delight viewers for miles around.

The Individual

By the year 2001 the changes brought by consciousness technology are seen most dramatically in the individual. Having been trained to develop their intuitive and creative powers of mind, individuals become more spontaneous and given to pursuing the kind of life that they really want. As more opportunities become available, most people find that they do not have to work at a boring job; that both fulfillment and financial security are possible.

Young people no longer strive to dress and act alike, but delight in their individuality. They outdo each other in wearing distinctive, colorful clothes that reflect their personalities and moods. The advent of new fabrics makes individually styled clothes relatively cheap to make and encourages new designs. Both boys and girls learn how to design their own clothes.

Young people now grow up with a strong belief in themselves and their inner destiny. They are persistent in achieving their goals, which they realize can be fulfilled only in the context of society. They develop extraordinary skills at co-operating in mutual efforts.

Those who come to their early twenties in the year 2001 may be the most idealistic generation the world has known. But they are also practical, since they know that their inner destinies can be accomplished only by actually doing what they believe in. They take psychic abilities for granted. Anyone who tries to show off by bending spoons is laughed at as immature. The ideal role model for these young people is the person who effortlessly blends his or her psychic and logical powers of mind to accomplish new ideas and actions that benefit the community.

The heroes of 2001 are the brilliant achievers in the arts, business, science, technology, government, industry and medicine. The younger the achiever, the more he or she is admired.

The most prized quality for the geniuses of 2001 is *balance*—between logic and intuition, between individuality and group responsibility, between ego and service, between imagination and practicality, between dignity and a sense of humor, between receiving love and giving love.

The youth of 2001 take responsibility for their lives and their future. They know that they will create the best of what they can foresee. They believe in the power of positive prophecy.

If these prophecies are fulfilled, it is we who can take the credit. If the flowers of the future bloom in a garden of Eden, it is we who will have planted them. Our generation is the guardian of destiny; we are the custodians of tomorrow.

Sources

The abbreviation *RIP* refers to *Research in Parapsychology*, the annual proceedings of the Parapsychological Association, published by Scarecrow Press, 52 Liberty St, PO Box 4167, Metuchen, NJ 08840. *RIP* is the most complete source of current research in parapsychology. The Parapsychological Association is the official scientific organization of parapsychology and is affiliated with the American Association for the Advancement of Science. Membership is restricted to active researchers and students, and numbers more than 300 members around the world. For information, contact: The Parapsychological Association, PO Box 12238, Research Triangle Park, North Carolina 27709, USA.

Chapter 1: Believing the Impossible
1. Evaluation of the *National Enquirer* psychics appears in *The Book of Predictions*, by David Wallenchinsky, Amy Wallace and Irving Wallace (New York: William Morrow, 1981), p. 403.

2. For my 1971 predictions see Frank Foster, 'Psychic Predictions Upsurge in Economy' in *National Enquirer*, 23 May 1971. Evaluation of the predictions is done by Henry Chase, 'Cracks in the Crystal Ball' in *Cheshire Herald*, [Connecticut] 27 December 1973.

3. Fortune-tellers are analyzed by Emily P. Cary, 'Telling on the Fortune-Tellers' in *Psychic*, Vol. 7, No. 5 (1976), pp. 34–6.

4. Andrew Greeley reports on his survey of psychic experience in 'Mysticism Goes Mainstream' in *American Health*, February 1987.

5. The Iceland experiment was performed by Erlendur Haroldsson, 'Reading Habits, Belief in ESP and Precognition, in *RIP 1975*, pp. 28–9.

Chapter 2: Training your Dream Tigers
6. The Bessent studies appear in Chapter 14, 'Dreaming of Things to Come' of *Dream Telepathy*, by Montague Ullman and Stanley Krippner with Alan Vaughan (New York: Macmillan, 1973; 2nd ed., McFarland, 1989).

7. *Living Your Dreams*, by Gayle Delaney (New York: Harper & Row, 1979).

Chapter 3: Experiments in Time
8. Senator Claiborne Pell comments on methods of suppressing scientific research in *Omni*, February 1988, p. 6

9. Richard C. Neville's elevator-predicting experiment appears in 'Some Aspects of Precognition Testing' in *RIP 1975*, pp. 26–32.

10. Helmut Schmidt's and J.B. Rhine's precognition experiments are summarized by Douglas Dean, 'Precognition and Retrocognition' in *Psychic Exploration*, by Edgar D. Mitchell and others, edited by John White (New York: Putnam's, 1974).

11. Charles Tart compares precognitive and same-time ESP studies in 'The Time Barrier: Precognition Does Not Work as Well as present-time ESP' in *RIP 1981*, pp. 10–12.

12. The SRI remote-viewing work is reported by Harold E. Puthoff and Russell Targ in 'A Perceptual Channel for Information Transfer Over Kilometer Distances' in *Proceedings of the IEEE*, Vol. 64 (1976), pp. 329–54. An overview of remote-viewing work by several labs is given by Robert G. Jahn, 'The Persistent Paradox of Psychic Phenomena: An Engineering Perspective' in *Proceedings of the IEEE*, Vol. 70, February 1982.

13. The SRI experiment with Hella Hammid appears in H.E. Puthoff and R. Targ, 'Precognitive Remote Viewing' in *RIP 1975*, pp. 37–40.

14. Brenda Dunne and John Bisaha summarized their research in 'Precognitive Remote Perception' in *RIP 1979*, p. 117, and are included in the survey by Jahn, 1982, above.

15. Gertrude Schmeidler and Michaeleen Maher, 'Judges' Impressions of the Nonverbal Behavior of Psi-Conducive and Psi-Inhibitory Experimenters' in *Journal of American Society for Psychical Research*, July 1981.

Chapter 4: Making Contact
16. Howard E. Goldfluss comments on psychics in *Omni*, July 1987, p. 6.

17. My British election prediction is reported by Herb Kretzmer, 'Mr Big—Ready to Lead Britain, Says Scholarly Prophet' in London *Daily Express*, 27 April 1974.

18. Weston Agor's annotations of my predictions for him are an update of 'Postscript' in *Intuitive Management* (Englewood Cliffs, New Jersey: Prentice-Hall, 1984), reprinted with permission of the author.

19. The experiment with Carol Liaros is reported by Douglas Dean, 'A Precognitive Method for Testing Sensitives' in *RIP 1972*, pp. 97–9.

20. Jule Eisenbud, 'A Transatlantic Experiment in Precognition with Gerard Croiset' in *Journal of The American Society for Psychical Research*, Vol. 67, No. 16 (1973), pp. 1–25.

Chapter 5: Guiding Images
21. Eleanor Friede is quoted in 'Profiles in Business' in *Psychic*, Vol. 6, No. 1 (1974), p. 30.

Chapter 6: The Art of Prophecy
22. British journalist Peregrine Worsthorne speculates on Edward Kennedy in 'The Fate of the Dynasty' in the London *Sunday Telegraph*, 9 June 1968.

23. *California Superquake, 1975–1977?* by Paul James (Hicksville, New York: Exposition Press, 1974).

24. *We Are the Earthquake Generation*, by Jeffrey Goodman (New York: Berkeley Books, 1979)

25. *Pole Shift* by John White (New York: Doubleday, 1980).

Chapter 8: Making Prophecy Practical
25. Cayce's general accuracy is determined by Edgar Evans Cayce and Hugh Lynn Cayce, *The Outer Limits of Edgar Cayce's Power* (New York: Harper & Row), pp. 19–24.

26. Cayce's accuracy in earth-change predictions is determined by Mark A. Thurston, *Visions and Prophecies for a New Age* (Virginia Beach, Virginia: ARE Press, 1981), p. 27.

27. The consensus experiment's raw data appear in Steve Rubenstein, 'Bay Area Psychics' Early Line on 1977', 1 January 1977, and 'How the Bay Area Psychics Fared in '77', 2 January 1978, *San Francisco Chronicle*.

28. Alan Vaughan, 'The Psychics on President Ford,' in *Psychic*, Vol. 6, No. 3 (August 1975), p. 15.

29. James C. Carpenter, 'An Elaboration of the Repeated-Guessing Technique for Enhancing ESP Information Efficiency' in *RIP 1981*, p. 111.

30. Stephan A. Schwartz, *The Alexandria Project* (New York: Delacorte/Friede, 1982).

31. Stephan A. Schwartz and Randall J. De Mattei, *The Caravel Project: Final Report* (Los Angeles: Mobius Society, 1987).

Chapter 9: The Science of Prediction
32. Lee Harrison, 'Fancy New Computers, but Today's Weathermen Are No Better than 20 Years Ago' in *National Enquirer*, 24 April 1984.

33. John Latta, 'Stock Market Is Just Like Vegas—Pure Gambling' in *National Enquirer*, 30 July 1985.

34. Peter Grossman, 'The Superstar Analysts: Are They Really That Good?' in *Financial World*, December 1980.

35. J. Scott Armstrong, 'The Seer-Sucker Theory: The Value of Experts in Forecasting' in *Technology Review*, 83: 18–24, June/July 1980.

36. Erik Larson, 'Did Psychic Powers Give Firm a Killing in the Silver Market?' in *Wall Street Journal*, 22 October 1984.

37. 'Volunteers Predict Silver Futures in ESP Study,' in *Brain-Mind Bulletin*, Vol. 12, 11 August 1987.

38. Harold E. Puthoff, 'ARV (Associational Remote Viewing) Applications' in *RIP 1984*, pp. 121–2.

39. Robert Magnuson, 'Analysis of 1981 Economic Forecasts' in *Los Angeles Times*, 3 January 1982.

40. *The Book of Predictions*, op. cit., note 1.

41. David Loye, 'The Brain and the Future' in *The Futurist*, October 1982, p. 19.

42. The book *Executive ESP*, by Douglas Dean and John Mihalasky, is edited by Sheila Ostrander and Lynn Schroeder (Englewood Cliffs, New Jersey: Prentice-Hall, 1974).

43. Weston Agor's survey appears in *Intuitive Management*, op. cit., note 18.

44. William Keeler is quoted in 'Profiles in Business' in *Psychic*, Vol. 6, No. 1 (1974), p. 27.

45. *Profiles of the Future*, by Arthur C. Clarke (New York: Harper & Row, 1963; rev. ed., 1987).

46. Robert Silverberg is quoted by Michael Robertson, 'There is No Crystal Ball' in *San Francisco Chronicle*, 8 July 1980.

Chapter 10: The Flexible Future
47. Frances Vernier's premonition is reported under the title, 'Woman's Amazing Psychic Dream Saves 39 from Fiery Death' in *The Star*, 7 April 1981.

48. William G. Braud's formal report appears as 'Project Chicken Little: A Precognition Experiment Involving the Skylab Space Station' in *European Journal of Parapsychology*, Vol. 3, No. 2 (1980), pp. 149–65.

Chapter 11: Shaping your Future
49. The Santa Barbara studies are reported by Robert L. Morris, 'The Airport Project: A Survey of the Techniques for Psychic Development Advocated by Popular Books' in *RIP 1978*, pp. 54–6; and by Robert L. Morris, Michael Nanko and David Phillips, 'Intentional Observer Influence Upon Measurements of a Quantum Mechanical System' in *RIP 1978*, pp. 146–50.

50. The Yale study is reported by Ariel Levi, 'The Influence of Imagery and Feedback on PK Systems' in *RIP 1979*, pp. 57–8.

51. The Simonton work is summarized by Judith Glassman, 'They Beat Cancer' in *Family Circle*, Vol. 94, No. 3 (24 February 1981), p. 59.

52. The quote from Ben Bova is from his 'The Role of Science Fiction' in *Science Fiction, Today and Tomorrow*, edited by Reginald Bretnor (Baltimore, Maryland: Penguin Books, 1975), p. 7, with permission of the author.

53. Roy Amara is quoted (in condensed form), from his 'The Futures Field: Searching for Definitions and Boundaries' in *The Futurist*, Vol. 15, No. 1 (1981), pp. 25–9.

Chapter 12: Time Will Tell
54. Experimental tests of my theory are published in my report, 'The Meaning of Coincidence' in *Parapsychology Review*, Vol. 11, No. 4 (1980), pp. 9–12, available from the Parapsychology Foundation, 228 East 71st Street, New York, NY 10021, USA.

55. Robert G. Jahn and Brenda Dunne discuss the philosophical implications of their work in *Margins of Reality: The Role of Consciousness in the Physical World* (New York: Harcourt, Brace, Jovanovich, 1988).

Psychic Reward

Intuition Training Software

Created by Alan Vaughan and Jack Houck, *Psychic Reward* software teaches 89 per cent of people to improve psychic skills with practice—with trainees averaging a 17 per cent increase in ESP scores.

Psychic Reward is an electronic wheel of fortune with 96 per cent positive feedback. You predict which of the wheel's 26 lettered slots, A–Z, will be chosen by the computer as the random target. The closer you get to the target, the higher you score in money points. This sensitive feedback design teaches you how to predict the future (precognition) and make your predictions come true (psychokinesis).

The most sophisticated intuition training system ever developed, *Psychic Reward* is a precision test instrument that automatically records and analyzes scores. A chart records your progress over three series of 20 tests with 30 trials each (1,800 trials in total). An analysis program gives the odds against chance for your increase in scoring from first to last series—giving proof of your ESP learning.

IBM compatible or Macintosh. IBM uses color monitor or Hercules graphics card for monochrome monitor. Available from Alan Vaughan, Mind Technology Systems, 3223 Madera Ave., Los Angeles, CA 90039, USA. Tel: (213) 666-7243.

About the Author

Alan Vaughan is an internationally known psychic researcher and intuitive. He is rated America's most successful predictor by the Central Premonitions Registry. His first book, *Patterns of Prophecy*, was acclaimed as 'a great contribution to psychic understanding'. Previous books recently reissued are *Incredible Coincidence* and *Dream Telepathy*.

The author has taught psychic techniques to thousands of people over the last 20 years. His research began in 1967 with a grant from the Parapsychology Foundation to study the precognitive abilities of England's finest mediums. He has worked with many psychic research centers, currently the Mobius Society, which rates him 86 per cent accurate in ESP experiments. Holding an honorary doctorate in parapsychology, he has been affiliated with the Parapsychological Association since 1969 and is listed in *Who's Who in America*.

Editor of two magazines, *Psychic* and *Reincarnation Report*, he has been written about in over 20 books and has published in such magazines as *Omni, Analog, The Futurist* and *Fate*. He has made many media appearances in the U.S. ('20/20') and England ('Nova') as an expert or precognition. Currently he is developing a TV series on paranormal themes. He lives with his wife and three children in Los Angeles.

Index

Of further interest . . .

Miracles

A Scientific Exploration of Wondrous Phenomena

D. Scott Rogo

In the first scientific, comprehensive and critical investigation of miraculous phenomena, D. Scott Rogo, one of the world's most widely published experts on parapsychology, documents and examines hundreds of remarkable instances of levitation, bleeding stigmata, miraculous images and visions, weeping statues, bilocating saints, and many lesser known but equally impressive cases.

Yet *Miracles* is more than just a compilation of wonders. Drawing on both conventional science and the most recent findings of parapsychology laboratories throughout the world, the author demonstrates that miracles are actually generated by the formidable powers of the human mind itself. But can this explanation be reconciled with the belief that miracles are exclusively religious phenomena? The book's conclusions are challenging and provide some surprising theories about the nature of supernatural involvement in the miraculous.

For the student of the paranormal or anyone who is curious about these little-understood events, this new and updated edition of *Miracles* makes compelling reading, a thorough and accessible inquiry into an astonishing subject.